SON OF VIRGINIA

A Life in America's Political Arena

L. DOUGLAS WILDER

Guilford, Connecticut

An imprint of Rowman & Littlefield

Distributed by NATIONAL BOOK NETWORK

British Library Cataloguing in Publication Information Available

Library of Congress Cataloging-in-Publication Data Available

ISBN 978-1-4930-1083-7 (hardback)
ISBN 978-1-4930-1952-6 (e-book)

∞™ The paper used in this publication meets the minimum requirements of American National Standard for Information Sciences—Permanence of Paper for Printed Library Materials, ANSI/ NISO Z39.48-1992.

For my mother, Beulah Olive Wilder

CONTENTS

CHAPTER ONE

Carry Me Back

"You've done it now. You will never go any further." This was the verdict from my close friends. Imagine what my detractors were saying.

It was 1970. I was newly elected to the Virginia State Senate, representing Richmond as the first African American senator since Reconstruction, and I'd been on the job for only three weeks when people thought I had all but destroyed my political future.

Most people thought the very fact I'd been elected was a shock to the system, and it would probably be best if I stayed under the radar for a while.

Well, it was not to be. Shortly after the election, my wife and I went up to Northern Virginia for a political retreat. At the very end of it, a musical group got up and began performing the state song, "Carry Me Back to Old Virginny." Just to be clear, the song is a romantic ode to slavery—there's just no other way to look at it:

> Carry me back to old Virginny,
> There's where the cotton and the corn and tatoes grow,
> There's where the birds warble sweet in the springtime,
> There's where the old darkey's heart am long'd to go,
> There's where I labor'd so hard for old massa,

Day after day in the field of yellow corn,
No place on earth do I love more sincerely
Than old Virginny, the state where I was born.

Carry me back to old Virginny,
There let me live 'till I wither and decay,
Long by the old Dismal Swamp have I wander'd,
There's where this old darkey's life will pass away.
Massa and missis have long gone before me,
Soon we will meet on that bright and golden shore,
There we'll be happy and free from all sorrow,
There's where we'll meet and we'll never part no more.

My wife and I gaped at each other, and then we stood up and walked out of the hall and went back to our hotel. We got many calls that night, folks asking, "Is everything okay? Is your wife ill?" The next day I told inquirers that I was just unnerved by the song. "But it's the state song," they argued. So it was. I knew that song, as we'd been taught to sing it in school, but for some reason it had escaped my notice that it was the official state song. It horrified me, but even my black friends were unsympathetic to my indignation. "People don't mean anything by it," one person told me. "You have to get this out of your system."

So we came back to Richmond, and that following Tuesday, I went to an event at the John Marshall Hotel, and as sure as the sun would rise, at the end of the evening, they launched into it again: "Carry me back to old Virginny."

I mumbled, "My, God," got up, and walked out for the second time in a week. I was upset. I drove around Richmond for an hour, trying to get myself together, and I just couldn't shake the overwhelming feeling that I had to do something about that song. Was I crazy? Suicidal? I had never been one to posture or raise a hue and cry. But those *words*.

I found the second stanza of the song particularly galling. The slave was saying he longed to die in Virginia and be reunited in heaven with "old massa and missis" where they'll be "happy and free from all sorrow." Good God, did he long to be a slave in heaven?

The next day, in my first speech on the floor of the Virginia State Senate, I stood in the chamber and announced, "We can ill afford the luxury of coining into song, phrase, or what have you, words which by their very construction recall the memories of our shameful history." My fellow senators sat in silence. You could hear a pin drop in the chamber, the cool reception masked an underlying dismay and even outrage.

I felt justified in my position. As legislators, how could we cut the political pie fairly when we couldn't get past the hardened crust, which in this instance was the unyielding vestige of racism? There wasn't another state song in the entire South that romanticized—or even mentioned—slavery. Looking at the matter broadly, I believed that Virginia's anthem failed the test of a good state song, which was to elevate and celebrate the special greatness of a state. For that reason, I introduced a bill, the first bill I ever sponsored, to abolish the Virginia state song.

I could never have predicted the passion of the protests and the public dissent that followed. Suddenly, instead of being embraced into the senate as the first African American, I was at the epicenter of a heated controversy. My family bore the brunt of it. My kids were ostracized at school, and they didn't understand why. I told them, in the same way my mother had tried to explain segregation on the public streetcars to me, that "this is something that will change" and they had nothing to be concerned about. I did my best to calm their fears, explaining that their father was a public official, and with that role came rights and responsibilities. It was a difficult period, but in truth the controversy only emboldened me.

On the editorial page of the *Richmond News Leader*, a scathing review appeared:

> *One cannot help but be saddened by this bit of news, for of course the song to which he objects is the State anthem. . . . To be sure, the song refers to slavery—one of the most lamentable aspects of Virginia's history. But slavery was not something that the Negro should be ashamed*

of; the Negro was not the enslaver. Slavery was a period of faith and courage and fortitude on the part of the Negro, a period of patience. He suffered it. He endured it. He emerged strong.

Many letters echoed this point, as if I were implying that African Americans should be ashamed of slavery—utter nonsense and in itself a romanticism of slavery, casting the slave as a courageous warrior when, in fact, he was the victim of a terrible practice. Slaves were not patient; they were trapped. Some emerged stronger; others were devastated, tortured, torn from their families, ruined, and murdered. Some had faith; others knew the kind of despair we can only imagine in our nightmares. It might have given comfort to some people to see the evils of slavery in such a noble light, but I wasn't buying it. Furthermore, anyone who gave this justification for keeping the song wasn't paying attention to the words. The former slave's voice in the song is sad and nostalgic, not victorious. Growing up in Virginia, I had always been struck by the fact that in the pictures I'd seen depicting slavery, the sun was always shining, the fields were always green, and the slaves were always sitting contentedly under lush trees at the plantation house. This convenient fiction undoubtedly helped to soothe many guilty consciences.

The *Richmond News Leader*, along with many others, also pointed out that "Carry Me Back to Old Virginny" was written by James Bland, an African American man. Bland had never been a slave—he was born free in New York. He wrote many songs, among them "In de Evening by de Moonlight" and "Oh, Dem Golden Slippers," and traveled with a minstrel show. It was said that the inspiration for "Carry Me Back to Old Virginny" grew out of his encounters with former slaves who were homesick for the South. I always figured he'd written the songs he knew would sell. In any case, the fact that the author was African American did not exonerate the song, although it was a convenient justification. I was told time and again that I was trying to bring shame on one of the nation's most prolific and beloved African American songwriters. Surely, as an African American myself, I would want one of my fellows to receive acknowledgment! And wasn't it wonderful—and a sign of Virginia's progress—that it had chosen a state song written by a person of my race? The fact that an African American wrote the song meant nothing to me.

The letters poured into my office. Some were supportive, most not. I learned how many contortions people could bend themselves into to defend the indefensible. Some messages were outright vulgar, such as the report declaring "Scientists Say Negro Still in Ape Stage" or the tract from the Ku Klux Klan. But most people were just making the point that we should put the past behind us. Some accused me of being a trouble-maker and said this was the kind of thing that happened when African Americans got into office.

Yes, it is true that back then it may have been "horrid and shameful" because Negroes then were not treated well. Some were, some were not. But the Negro has come quite a long way since then. I'm afraid that it is just you type of negro that makes "whiteys" so mad.

Not even a black likes a big mouth nigger!

You and all negroes should study the life of George W. Carver, Booker T. Washington and James Bland. They worked and accomplished something good for mankind. You just leave our State Song alone and work for the future of Virginia and the human race.

What in the world is your trouble that you do not like your State song? I should think you would be flattered that Va used one of a colored person's songs for their State song. Don't be so envious for God does not like envious people. . . . Now be a nice man like God would like you to be and please accept Carry Me Back to Old Va.

Some tried to make the astonishing point that although slavery was bad, the condition of African Americans would have been much worse had our people been left in Africa.

5

The senator might well reflect upon the fact that while no fair minded human being could possibly condone slavery, yet except for his forebears having been brought from Africa to this country in the slave trade, he himself and millions of others in his race, would still be suffering the sad lot of today's African blacks.

It would seem to me your history would have been much worse had the Negro not been brought to America as they were.

Somewhere along the way your ancestors virginity was entirely subjected to the white race. Who has ever seen a thorough negro with ginger color in his skin? You should be glad and proud of that because with your regular features, etc., it is the only reason you have gotten to be Senator.

Another writer scrawled on a copy of the *News Leader* editorial, "Wilder, you poor, stupid fool! Remember, there is always a boat to Africa awaiting you at the dock. Write an African song when you arrive!"

Through it all, I was quite aware that much of the response was a manner of backlash against a decade of rapid progress for African Americans, which, to be fair, involved some radical changes—and some even more radical voices. The 1960s had just come to a close, and many people were reeling. Even so, their fury at my position could be quite revealing and a sure sign that we had a long way to go—as this piece from the *Richmond Progress-Dixiecrat* so vividly demonstrates:

Mr. Wilder's unreasoned tirade is but the latest event in a series of tragic racial misunderstandings which began when we, the good White People of the South, graciously recognized the limited progress which the colored have made in recent decades and began voluntarily and enthusiastically allowing the darkies to assume such luxuries as the right to sit in the front of the bus and to share our water fountains and rest rooms with us.

This was an extreme although not entirely unusual response to my bill. Others tried to be more evenhanded. For example, a lot of people thought I objected to the word "darky" and figured the solution was to fix the song. One man suggested that the melody was pleasant, so we should conduct a lyric-writing contest for high school students to replace the words. And although my bill never made it out of committee, people spent years trying to come up with a new version, a new song, a new verse—a process I was not interested in.

To be fair, not all letters were against my bill, although most were. As one man wrote, quite poignantly, in support,

> I, like you, find the state song, "Carry Me Back to Ol Virginia" hyper-insulting to blacks and all progressive thinking citizens. In my opinion, anything that seeks to glorify the unfortunate and absurd institution of slavery should best be left to the regrettable past. It disturbs me a great deal to see slavery and the "noble southern cause" continually exalted and dignified as one of America's finest hours.

I responded to all letters. To my detractors, I wrote, "Though you have indicated you disagreed with what I was attempting to do, I wanted you to know that I respect your view. All that I ask of you is that you share the same respect for my view as I for yours. We then would have affected a mini-milestone of progress." To my supporters, I responded, "It has been stated that 'all that is required for evil to triumph is for good men to remain silent.' The 'plantation mentality' would indeed continue to haunt us, eventually to our graves, if those of us who have a responsibility to demand what is right and to criticize what is wrong fail to do so." Yet the debate continued on for decades. In 1994, long after I had moved on from the senate, a bill was introduced to replace several words in the song:

> "Darkey's" would be changed to "dreamer's."
> "old Massa" would be replaced with "my loved ones."

"Massa" would be replaced with "Papa."
"Missis" would be replaced with Mamma."

This whitewashing effort was tantamount to addressing a rotting foundation by painting the shutters. In any case, the bill failed to pass.

In 1997, the effort to replace the song gained new momentum. "Carry Me Back to Old Virginny" was declared the state song emeritus, as if conferring retirement with full honors, while the state scrambled to come up with an official replacement. Over the years, contests were held and many songs proposed and rejected, but a replacement has never been found, and our emeritus song remains Virginia's only official song in the minds of many. To this day, the controversy rages on.

To my knowledge, after my objection, that song was not sung publicly at official events in Virginia. It proved to me that positive results can be achieved even when the perceived objective, the passing of a bill to repeal the song, never came close to succeeding. That lesson has always stayed with me.

In those early days, my greatest supporters thought I'd doomed myself. That didn't come to pass, but even if it had, I would not have minded. I didn't need the job. I didn't seek public office to better myself financially. I had a very good law practice. The principle mattered to me. It was my first test in politics. And as my mother always told me, "It'll work out. You just make certain that you can see yourself straight."

❧

My initial act as an elected official, considered bold by many, might seem less foolhardy if you consider that my paternal grandparents were slaves. My father, Robert Judson Wilder, wasn't born a slave, but his older siblings were. My mother, Beulah Olive Richards, was born to free blacks in Charles City County, east of Richmond. My father's parents, James and Agnes Johnson Wilder, were slaves in nearby Goochland County. I never met my grandparents, but the fact that they were slaves was always intriguing to me. My father, who was a quiet and taciturn man, didn't want to talk about it. My mother would gently pressure him, "Douglas is asking questions, Robert. Tell him." And he would, reluctantly.

My grandparents were born into slavery—James in 1838 and Agnes in 1839. Little is known of their upbringing. I imagine they kept better records of thoroughbred racehorses and purebred dogs on plantations in those days. It would have been nice had there also been formal records of the people who happened to be slaves who were helping to build this nation.

My grandparents were also married in slavery. What prologue led to their union? Like so many African American families, what could not be remembered and passed on by older relatives is difficult, if not impossible, to piece together. It's not that we don't want to know. In many cases, we just can't. We'll never know with 100 percent certainty from what exact soil James and Agnes grew. My father never talked about anything he may have heard from his parents about the years they were slaves. He always looked ahead—planned what was next, as Wilders still are wont to do.

However, the family does have James and Agnes's marriage certificate. It shows that they were joined in holy matrimony at Braggs Farm, a plantation in Henrico County, Virginia, on April 25, 1856. As slaves were not allowed to officially marry, it is a decidedly informal document. It was signed by a "Mea Wilder," and that's how the name Wilder was adopted for our family. James and Agnes had two children in slavery and eleven more after they were freed. My father, born in 1886, was the second youngest.

As was common practice, my grandparents were sold to separate owners, in Richmond and Ashland, but unlike many slave families that were permanently torn apart, they lived close enough that my grandfather could visit my grandmother on Sundays, walking over twenty miles each way. He didn't have permission to do this—he just took off. The overseer knew what he was doing and fully understood that he wasn't running away. But the overseer had to do his job, so when my grandfather returned, he would get a whipping. Finally, the overseer realized that it was pointless to whip my grandfather every week. So he concocted a scheme, God love him, by which he beat a saddle with a whip and told my grandfather to holler as if he were being whipped.

My father recounted that when the Union soldiers approached Virginia in the dying days of the Civil War, all the slaves believed they were going to be killed by the soldiers. For days, as the entrance of Ulysses Grant's troops into the city became inevitable, Richmond's newspapers had been filled with stories of their brutality and immorality. All of Richmond was warned to be ready to face the very worst atrocities ever to confront a community of people because Lucifer's own were on their way. James's master and his overseer made sure the slaves on the plantation were well aware of the terrible fate that awaited them if Federal troops moved into and gained control of central Virginia. The slaves, having no independent source of information, believed it and hid in a tobacco silo as the city was set on fire. My grandfather nearly suffocated before breaking out to discover that the Union soldiers were not his murderers but his liberators. Richmond was torched by fleeing Confederate soldiers, not by the Union army.

Once my grandparents were freed, they settled into life in Richmond, working hard and raising their family. James was twenty-eight and Agnes twenty-seven. They had lived lifetimes before emancipation, but they were only getting started. They might have come from slavery, but they did not allow that to be their identity. They were people who respected education and yearned for their children to be educated. They were driven people, they were family people, they were home owners. They were part of the American Dream—Lincoln's emancipated American Dream. They fought to change America by refusing to be anything other than Americans. My grandfather was a teamster. He had his own wagon and sold meal and took care of horses.

Incredibly for the era, the two managed to build and own a home across the street from what would become our family home at 933 N. 28th Street in Richmond. When I take time to think about that, it amazes me. The times were not conducive to any man with a full brood of children building and owning a house—never mind one merely years removed from servitude. I bet just a few years prior to their stepping into their own home, James and Agnes couldn't have imagined it, either. But as best I can tell, it didn't occur to them to dwell on their former lives. They just got busy raising a family on a little square of land that would shelter several generations of Wilders for decades to come.

My grandparents were very devout, and my grandfather was a deacon and trustee of the First African Baptist Church, one of the largest churches in the world. They built a life for their family, and I am the lucky recipient of their devotion. That ancestry, so recently experienced and so close up and personal, imposed upon us a certain obligation that I never forgot.

I was born January 17, 1931, the seventh of eight children. I had six sisters and one brother. Two other children had died before I was born—a daughter, Ruth, the oldest of all the siblings, who died at three years old of pneumonia, and a son who died shortly after birth.

I had a big name for a little boy: Lawrence Douglas—although my mother always called me Douglas. When I was quite young, I asked my mother where I got my name. She explained what large shoes I had to fill. Lawrence was after Paul Laurence Dunbar. My birth certificate has it spelled Laurence, but because it was so often misspelled in school, I started spelling it in the more common way as Lawrence. My mother told me he was a great author and poet. Douglas was after Frederick Douglass, the great orator and abolitionist. "He was a slave," she said, "and then he fought against slavery."

My eyes grew big. "He was a slave?" I asked.

"Yes," she said, "just like your father's parents. These two men rose above it. One was a great writer, and the other was a great orator. And if you're going to be named after them, you've got to measure up."

Measuring up—and especially the value of education—had a long legacy in my family. When my grandmother was a slave in Ashland, she cared for the household's children. Each time the tutors came to teach, grandmother sat in the room with her sewing and learned right along with them—reading, writing, and arithmetic—and then taught her own children. So while education was illegal for slaves, they had a desire to learn, and they did learn.

I was always impressed that even before emancipation, the value of education was being sewn into the essence of the Wilder family's being. My mother was a learned woman, fierce about education. She was born in Charles City, Virginia, in 1892 and never knew her natural father. Early in her life, her mother, Mary Richards, brought her to Richmond to live with her grandmother, but the pair didn't stay long. They moved to Newark, New Jersey, where Mary found work as a housekeeper. She also found a husband, Robert Tolan. He was the chauffeur of the family for whom both of them worked.

Tolan treated my mother as if she were his own child. She always described him as a wonderful man who was good to her and her mother. My mother always talked fondly of her time in New Jersey, where she excelled in an integrated school system. Then everything changed in the worst way it could for a child barely entering high school. My grandmother Mary was diagnosed with cancer. My mother was only fourteen when she watched her mother succumb. She had lost both her parents and most of her already small family.

Unable to help my mother grow into a young woman, Tolan sent her back to Richmond to live with her two remaining known relatives, her grandmother and Mary's sister, Kate Watkins. We came to know her as Aunt Kate. Tolan never forgot my mother, though. He stayed in contact during the years, always sending little cards and gifts around holidays and on birthdays.

My mother graduated from Richmond's segregated high school system in 1909. She had ambitions to be a journalist. She would have been a good one. An excellent writer who loved words, my mother had an impressive command of the English language. She was the best crossword puzzle solver I'd ever met. In her daily life, she spoke colloquially, but she knew words. She had an enormous vocabulary, and she could completely solve the Sunday *New York Times* crossword puzzle, getting upset with herself if she missed a single clue. She'd call out to me, "Give me a four-letter word that means . . . ," and in this way, she drew me in to the love of language.

My Aunt Kate, who had helped raise my mother, was not an educated woman, but she was a devout woman, and she made a great impression on us. She would host what she called silver teas, which meant that people put silver in the plate—not pennies but nickels and dimes. She'd ask my mother to volunteer her children to perform at these teas, and we'd recite poetry, sing songs, play the piano, or otherwise perform. I never sang at those teas, but I performed bits from plays or speeches. The teas taught us to have a public presence and hold our own in the world. Often, others in attendance asked our mother to volunteer us for their own events, which she did.

Expectations were high, and they were repeated on a daily basis. We were expected to conduct ourselves well and learn to be productive and self-reliant. The worst sin on earth was to be a laggard. My mother made me believe that I was the greatest little boy in the world, capable of doing anything I set my heart on.

My father was a salesman for the Southern Aid Life Insurance Company, the oldest black-owned insurance company in the country. His early dream had been to be a lawyer. The understanding was that his brother Charles would become a doctor with my father's help, and then Charles would help my father with his education. When Charles became a doctor, it was a phenomenal achievement for the son of former slaves. But on Christmas Day 1925, at the age of thirty, Charles died, just as he began practicing medicine. My father was never able to realize his dream. His brother's death crushed his aspirations. He had a house full of children who needed his care and support, so he stayed with the insurance company. He started as a salesman and moved up to a supervisor, but he never went far. He worked at that same company until he retired, never making more than about fifty bucks a week. But we got by, and my father never asked anyone for anything. He came home for lunch every single day, taking a streetcar from wherever in the city he was working.

We lived in what I've often called a "gentle" poverty, in the segregated neighborhood of Church Hill. We were taught to be proud of our neighborhood, which was rich with American history. Patrick Henry gave his "Give me liberty or give me death" speech at the St. John's Episcopal Church there, and the neighborhood was named after that church. Many of the homes were old, dating back to before the Civil War. But ours was new. My father had a house built for us by an African American contractor named Jeb Bailey. His daughter, Ethel Bailey Furman, the first African American architect licensed in Virginia, drew the plans. As a woman and not being white, her professional life hadn't been easy, but she kept at it. The lesson from her life was clear: If you have strikes against you, you don't argue or fuss, you just do what has to be done and persevere. I still have the contract for the house. It cost $2,500—one-third at signing and the rest on completion. No banks were involved.

Our home was a seven-room corner lot structure with four bedrooms and a bath, and my father believed in having the right things. We always had enough space in our house and as many amenities as we could afford. We had an angora cat and a collie or spitz, all purebred. We also had canaries and goldfish. We had a grape arbor and fruit trees in our backyard, along with a stable, which was used as a barn. We had two hundred homing pigeons (thus squab on occasion for breakfast), sitting hens with fresh eggs, geese, ducks, turkeys, and even guinea hens. The stable also housed workhorses that my father leased to men with vegetable carts or meal wagons.

As financially strapped as he was, my father believed in uplift and improvement. He had a piano in the house, and all of us were expected to take lessons. My sister Naomi played well, but my other sisters opted to sing in choral groups. My brother was completely disinterested. I, on the other hand, loved playing the piano. I took lessons, paid for by my father at some meager price, afforded by one of his coworkers, a music scholar, who taught to supplement his income. I excelled in the lessons. My mother insisted that I practice immediately upon coming home from school and later confessed how much she loved to hear me play in the afternoons.

My dad was quite a figure in the community. He had a way about him—a dignity and intellect that made people seek his counsel. I can still remember the way he'd stand on the porch and look down on the supplicants from a high perch. He was five feet seven inches, but his deep, booming voice and his elevated position on the porch made him seem larger. He had a singer's resonance, and he was a bass baritone, performing with the Sabbath Glee Club. They traveled the country for performances and recorded songs such as "Somebody's Watching at Your Door." I always remember the way my father demanded respect, even from whites. He was never subservient. He had dignity. He never left the house without being properly attired and wearing a necktie or a bow-tie and a used Homburg hat, though you couldn't tell it was used. He dressed as if he were somebody, and he *was* somebody. That was a strong lesson of my childhood—you had to *be* the person you wanted others to respect.

At home, my father was a strict disciplinarian who didn't tolerate bickering or grumbling. "Whatever you have, you're better off than I was when I was born," he'd tell us if we expressed unhappiness. "I don't want to hear any complaints." Although I would sometimes chafe at his stern demeanor, as any child would, when I got older and learned about his history as the son of freed slaves, I cut him some slack. I could not even imagine the confusing and troubling context of his life, and it made me admire him more when I understood his upbringing. I suppose one might say, "But it was wonderful. His parents were free!" Yet I often contemplate the way it must have been for them, feeling the lingering effects of slavery. I imagine it was a form of posttraumatic stress to go on in life after they were freed. And the effects of that bitter heritage lived on in their children. My father was a very good and responsible man, but he could never allow himself to be carefree. There was an edge to him that endured until his death.

I didn't have a close relationship with my father, but I worshipped my brother Bob, who was ten years older than me. My mother thought my adoration of Bob approached idolatry. She used to say, "You think he's Jesus Christ!" I copied him in everything he did. What he liked I liked. It got so bad that when Bob announced that he hated potatoes, I said I hated them too. Nothing my mother said would convince me to eat potatoes. He also threw away the tip of the ice cream cone, and for years I didn't eat the tip of an ice cream cone because Bob said so.

Bob took me under his wing, and he let me accompany him when he hung out with his friends, delivered newspapers, or played sports. The older kids didn't like me being around, but Bob shrugged it off. "He's my brother," he'd say. "He can be here if I'm here." Bob knew how things were on the street, and because I was small, he wanted me to be tough. He taught me to box guys who were bigger and older, and sometimes I'd come home bloodied, and our mother would be upset. But we didn't stop. My brother told me that once you get in a tussle with a kid who's older and you knock him down, he'll tell the world, and people will know you mean business.

The saddest day of my young life was when Bob left home, being drafted in World War II to join the army and serve with the First Cavalry, leaving me with a house full of women. He wore a dressy uniform with riding pants and spurs. He was such a handsome guy—five feet ten inches with curly black hair and bronze skin. He was always popular with the girls. Upon discharge from the service, he eventually moved north and raised a family. He decided to go to the New England School of Photography in New Haven, Connecticut. His marriage ended in divorce, and he returned in later years to work and eventually retire in Richmond. Sadly, he died soon after retiring. I was the lieutenant governor of the state at the time, and a few months before he died, Bob wrote me a lovely letter, telling me what he thought of me. I cherish those words from my beloved brother. Tears filled my eyes as I read, "Sometimes I get up at night and think about how grateful I am to have a brother with such a heart." His approval meant everything to me.

My older sisters coddled me, and my younger sisters fought with me, in the way of most big families. My mother would chastise me, saying, "You cannot fight my girls," to which I would reply plaintively, "But your girls are ganging up on me!" There was a time when I was absolutely convinced that I did not belong in my family. "Did the stork bring me?" I asked my mother, and when she seemed to acknowledge it, I wanted to know, "Does the stork ever make a mistake?" I'd tell my sisters that I was in the wrong place, that I was meant for another home—perhaps one with a car and more money. "My real parents are coming to get me one day," I warned them. They thought that was hilarious.

My oldest sister, Naomi, was a schoolteacher and was there at home to correct and direct our attention to proper speech and decorum—although with my disciplinarian father, there was little need for any additional help in that regard. Our neighborhood had just about everything one could imagine. The blacksmith shop was right across the street. My father would send me over there to have a piece of iron forged into whatever he had in mind. It was my first opportunity to see the smithy drive nails into the horses' hoof coverings to put the shoes on. There was a hardware store on one corner and a printing shop on the other. There was a bakery and dry cleaner's one block away and a laundry two blocks away. The barbershop and icehouse were down the street. There was a restaurant across the street, with a shoe-shine parlor right next to it. There was a drugstore on the corner and a large lumberyard, a firehouse, and a pool hall nearby. There was another drugstore, several grocery stores, and a dance hall all within blocks. In addition, there was a department store and the "colored" movie house within two blocks of where I lived. Last but not least was the Fourth Baptist Church right across the street, a church that I went to quite frequently when I was late going to the family church. The streetcar line ended one block from our house.

Although we lived in segregation, our community was complete. Everything we needed was near at hand. The closeness of the community was like a warm embrace that kept us safe. And we needed that embrace because Harry Flood Byrd's Democratic Party organization ruled our world. Byrd was the most influential politician in Virginia's history, with an iron grip on every aspect of state life. His roots were deep; his ancestor, William Byrd II, had established the city of Richmond. And with all his power, it seemed that the meaning and purpose of Byrd's life was to maintain the status quo of a segregated state.

My father hated Byrd, and he had little respect for the state constitution. Virginia's constitution, written at the turn of the twentieth century, had a chilling purpose. Indeed, one of the document's prime movers was clear and unrelenting when he publicly stated its primary goal: "Discrimination! Why that is exactly what we propose; that is why this Convention was elected—to discriminate to the very extremity of permissible action under the limitations of the Federal Constitution with the view to the elimination of every Negro who can be gotten rid of—legally—without materially impairing the strength of the white electorate." The purveyors of this policy managed to successfully disenfranchise most African Americans and most poor white Virginians until the mid-1960s. Southern historian V. O. Key once wrote that, compared to Virginia, "Mississippi is a hotbed of democracy." Byrd embraced this dangerous code, and in my father's mind, Byrd was an uneducated man who spewed nonsense. In his "wisdom," Byrd tried to make sure that African Americans didn't get educated. My father, I now know, voted Republican, although back then he never told anyone, fearing retaliation. He used to say, "I believe in the Australian form of the ballot—secret."

It's significant that he was even voting during those years, when a poll tax was imposed to discourage the African American vote. My father was having none of it. He paid that tax and made sure his name was on the rolls. My mother didn't talk politics with my father, as he was of a mind that women's political opinions didn't matter. Although this attitude was not uncommon for the times, it was a shame. I don't believe I ever knew a brighter woman than my mother.

During my early years, I was hardly aware of racism because I rarely interacted with white people. But when I began riding streetcars around age five, I started waking up to reality. We lived at the end of the streetcar line, so the car would be empty when we got on. My mother would pull me toward the back, and I'd protest, wanting to sit near the front. She'd say, "No, let's go to the back." And I'd argue with her when she insisted.

"What's wrong?" I asked. "Why can't I sit here?" She never said it wasn't allowed or that it was racial. She'd just say, "I'll explain it to you later. Right now, this is what you have to do." And so I obeyed, reluctantly. But if I didn't understand then, I soon did because the rules of segregation were hard to miss. I began to see that there were ordinary places that were off limits to me, ordinary activities—such as trying on clothes at a department store—that weren't possible. I mulled over these inequities, and they weighed on me. Once, when I was older, I was asked to recite Thomas Jefferson's Declaration of Independence at a July Fourth celebration. I rehearsed with my mother at home, booming, "We hold these truths to be self-evident, that all men are created equal, that they are endowed by their Creator with certain unalienable rights, that among these are life, liberty, and the pursuit of happiness." At one point, I turned to my mother. "What does the word 'unalienable' mean?"

"It means a right no one can take from you," she replied.

"Well, does that Declaration of Independence apply to me?" I asked. She gave me a stern look. "Yes," she said. And when your mother tells you something and you love your mother, you believe her. I was so certain that my mother would never lie to me that I trusted her completely. And that in turn gave me the confidence to think of myself as an equal.

Mother never told any of us that we couldn't achieve at the highest possible level, but she always insisted we had to work harder to get it done. She'd say, "This will change. You'll see. What you need to do is be as smart as you can be—and be smarter than the next person." She wasn't afraid of our questions, our doubts, and our challenges—and I was adept at all of those things. I can say today that it was my good fortune to grow up in a household where asking "Why?" was encouraged. My mother stimulated us to have thoughts, to expand them and express them. She fortified my desire to read voraciously, to speak well, and to participate in the activities the "smart boys" did to showcase my abilities.

I started prekindergarten at a school in the West End of the city, Elba Elementary School. The neighborhood doctor, who was also our family doctor, Vernon J. Harris, had a daughter my age, Jean, and since we lived only two blocks apart, my mother asked if I could hitch a ride with Jean and her two cousins, which I did.

The next year, I was formally enrolled at George Mason Elementary School only two blocks from my home, and Jean and I started there. At George Mason Elementary, I ran my mouth all the time. I always wanted to show what I knew. I always wanted to be up front—to get the role of the prince or the king in a play so I could speak. I usually got the lead part, and Jean was always the princess or queen.

I was a ball of fire. If they'd had Ritalin back in the 1940s, I no doubt would have been diagnosed with attention-deficit/hyperactivity disorder. I was a very good student, always making As and always getting an equal number of demerits for either being late or furnishing the answers to questions being asked of other students. My teachers eventually had to discourage me from raising my hand in class because I couldn't stop myself from dominating the discussions. I never was concerned with homework because I would do that before I arrived home every day.

I lived in the glorious world of the mind, which was much better than the infrastructure of segregation. George Mason was a crumbling facility, as were all African American schools. We were lucky to get a tenth of the state money devoted to the pristine white schools. Our school was overcrowded and cold during the winter with no indoor toilets in several buildings. We had no cafeteria or auditorium and no regular school nurse. We had to make do with secondhand books that white students had previously used and meager supplies. This inequity was rarely discussed, and because we had no basis of comparison, we didn't know the extent of our disadvantage.

The principal was white, as was the case with all of the schools, elementary or high. The teachers were African American. They insisted not only on discipline but also on correctness in dress, speech, attitude, and general decorum.

My mother made certain that in our lunch bags, there was always a piece of fresh fruit (apple, pear, banana, or orange). That was every day—and quite a feat for a home of limited means during the time when I was growing up.

Church was the center of our lives, and it had a very strong influence on me. We attended the First African Baptist Church, where my father served as a deacon and a trustee just like his father before him. This was a marvelous historical church, more than one hundred years old when I was a child. It originally served both freed and slave blacks. Members numbered over two thousand. It was the largest African American church in Virginia.

We all had to go to Sunday school and attend church. And before we left for church, we listened to spirituals on the radio. I remember vividly every Sunday listening to the Wings Over Jordan Choir, which recorded the first national and international program by African Americans. Their theme song was "Go Down Moses . . . Let My People Go." Then we'd go to church, and the minister would inspire us and upbraid us and call on us to do better. He always spoke about the value of civility but at the same time not being satisfied with where you were. That made an impression on me. The church was also a social and political meeting place—whether it was a meeting of the National Association for the Advancement of Colored People (NAACP), a charity meeting, or a meeting to discuss how to improve the neighborhood or the plight of our people.

When I got to the seventh grade, I and four others in my class were skipped, and we had to complete only the first semester of seventh grade. At age thirteen, I was enrolled in the all-black Armstrong High School, starting in January. I was still very much interested in being a top student and made all As—but also the accompanying five demerits. Armstrong High was about three miles from home, and my father would give me the fare for one-half of the trip, so I'd have to walk either to or from school.

Jean Harris attended Armstrong High along with me. My dear childhood friend would later be the first African American admitted to and graduating from what was then known as the Medical College of Virginia, now part of Virginia Commonwealth University, where I teach. She had an illustrious career as a physician, an educator, an adviser to President Carter, and the first African American cabinet secretary to a governor in Virginia.

I was the only boy in the entire high school who still wore knickers. My father decreed that I couldn't wear long pants until I turned fourteen. Oh, how I suffered! What girl wanted to have anything to do with a boy in knickers? My sister Doris, who was next to the oldest, lived across the street from the school, so we arranged that I get a pair of long pants and change at her house. That was between us, and I was pleased to be "normal" and not the object of derision.

Although I loved football and wanted to play, I was considered too small and never went out for the team, confining myself to sandlot quarterbacking. I did get to be a cheerleader, the closest I got to the team, and that was the only athletic letter I ever earned.

I continued to do well in school and got good grades. I was excited about courses in science and biology but was attracted to history and English literature. I was particularly impressed by a course titled "Negro History" with J. R. Ransome, a pioneer in teaching black history in the schools. His father was an instructor at Virginia Union University, and I later took his class titled "Bible" in college. "Negro History" was not a required course but an elective; I have since questioned why it was not required.

In Ransome's high school class, we read a book called *The Story of the Negro Retold* by Carter G. Woodson, whom many considered the father of Negro history. I was enthralled to learn about Nat Turner's revolt in Southampton, Virginia, in 1831. I thought he was a giant among men. Yet whenever I read other accounts of his marauding massacre, he was described as a religious zealot. Having known about my own family ancestry, especially that my grandparents were slaves, I felt emotional when I learned more about the barbarity and inhumanity of the system of slavery in this country. Ransome was eloquent yet not emotional. He would ask such rhetorical questions as, "Why did slaves run away?," forcing us to think about how the slaves lived and what motivated their quest for freedom.

Many decades later, when the story of my election as governor of Virginia was included in the fourth-grade textbooks, I hoped it would provoke such thought and conversation.

Any mention of Patrick Henry to my father brought a lecture on the fact that Henry was known for speaking and not fighting, and he'd always lived rather comfortably in Hanover County. But Henry's "Give me liberty or give me death" speech and Jefferson's declaration that "all men are created equal" stirred in me irreconcilable conflicts between egalitarian posturing and the reality of actual existence.

World War II was under way and was coming to an end. I was consumed by the fight, especially since Bob was serving in Oahu, Hawaii. I followed the European theater of operations and eagerly consumed the news in the daily papers. I was particularly interested in accounts of the "Desert Fox," German General Erwin Rommel, as he was being pursued across the African deserts and finally defeated at El-Alamein in Egypt, signaling the beginning of the end for the Axis powers.

I always looked for examples in the war of heroics by people like me. One was a man named Dorie Miller. Miller was an African American working in the navy mess at Pearl Harbor. When the Japanese attacked, he heard people crying that the captain was injured on the bridge. Without pausing, Miller ran to the bridge and carried the captain to safety. He then returned and manned a machine gun (which he'd not been trained to use) and began firing at Japanese planes.

Miller survived the attack on Pearl Harbor but died two years later when his ship was bombed by a Japanese submarine. He was posthumously awarded the Navy Cross, its highest medal of honor, becoming the first African American to receive it. I was enthralled by Miller's patriotism and heroism, but I kept asking myself why he fought so valiantly for a nation that still considered him second class. That question continued with me even as I dealt with the enemy on the hills of Korea some few short years later.

I studied hard, but it was the neighborhood at large that polished my ambitions. A wonderful sense of community emanated from every corner. There was such love and caring. From the bakery to the barbershop to the grocery to the shoe shine to the laundry, everyone looked out for us, and we *belonged* to each other. We could go into anyone's home and eat! People would care for us as if we were their own.

The adults always kept up the pressure. Many times, people said to me, "I couldn't get an education myself. I had to drop out of school. Don't you end up like I did. You get smart. Don't pay any attention to people telling you things that you can't do."

By this time, I had started shining shoes in the parlor across the street, and I hung out at the barbershop. Dick Reid's Church Hill Barber Shop was literally a community center, and those guys took me under their wing. I commanded center stage in the barbershop and did everything I could to impress any and all with my learning. The owners encouraged me to speak and to explain, and they lamented, as did so many of the customers, that they had not been able to get through high school.

I enjoyed sharing what I'd learned, and they got a kick out of it. I'd bring in my encyclopedia, and they'd test my knowledge, getting a little betting pool going. It was fun for them, and it was good for me to hone my skills that way. I remember describing how the American entry into World War II started with the bombing of Pearl Harbor, and one guy said, "Oh no, it was in the Philippines." And then I explained, "Well, no, it was the Hawaiian archipelago." (I knew this because my brother Bob was stationed there.) The other guys looked up and said, "Listen to this kid. He knows what he's talking about." I won that bet and earned a dollar. They always encouraged me, and in the process, they enabled me to have a forum where I could express myself. Later, when I was in public office and a young person asked me how I became comfortable with the public stage, I referred fondly to the old barbershop.

There was a yellow book hanging on the wall with the names recorded of everyone who was registered to vote. Voting was taken very seriously, as it was a hard-won right. Along with other southern states, Virginia had a history of imposing poll taxes and literacy tests for blacks in order to "purify" the ballot box, so being registered to vote was a cherished and significant thing. Everyone talked politics at the barbershop, but it became a rule that if your name wasn't in the book, you didn't have a right to run your mouth. They appointed me the "sheriff." If someone had an opinion, I checked the book, and I was the one to say, "Your name isn't in that book, you can't talk."

In my junior year, my social life picked up, and I started being seriously involved with girls. I went to many dances and teen gatherings and was well accepted as "the boy from the other side of town." I had joined the cadet corps—similar to ROTC—and we had to buy our own uniforms and boots. My mother approved and helped me purchase them. I loved to put on my uniform in company drills, mostly because the girls liked cadets, and I liked girls. My first date was to escort a young lady to the cadet ball. She taught me the latest dance steps, and I emerged as quite fanciful with a step or two.

In 1947, when I was sixteen, my older sister belonged to a group that brought the famed Paul Robeson to perform at the Richmond Mosque. Robeson was a real hero. I had admired him in movies, and I was absolutely thrilled to go see him onstage. He was a great performer and had become an incredible orator and advocate for civil rights. Following the 1946 lynching of four African Americans in Georgia, he arranged a meeting with President Harry Truman. Robeson warned the president that if the government did not enact legislation to end lynching, "the Negroes will defend themselves." Insulted by Robeson's boldness and believing that the time was not right for anti-lynching legislation, Truman ended the meeting. Robeson did not stop there. He founded the American Crusade Against Lynching and took his campaign to the people.

At the Mosque, Richmond's largest indoor facility, Robeson stood up and said, "I look out and see that this audience is segregated. And I had promised I would never appear before another segregated audience." And he walked off the stage, leaving a packed house. The organizers raced out behind him and begged him to return. "Look, we'll have to give these people their money back. We're broke. This will break us!" And he came back because he didn't want to see the sorority hurt. I sat enthralled as he spoke and then did a musical performance. Seeing this man in the flesh, I understood for the first time the power a single human being can have to move an audience or a nation.

One day later that year, the guys at the barbershop were talking excitedly about Jackie Robinson, who had just been signed to play for the Brooklyn Dodgers. They were planning to ride up to New York on Saturday night so they could see him play in Sunday's game against the St. Louis Cardinals. Eyeing me thoughtfully, one of them said, "You're small enough to fit in the back. You can ride with us." I was in a state of delirious excitement, even though I was usually a fan of the Cardinals. We drove up to New York and took our seats in the stadium. And wouldn't you know it, that was the game when one of my baseball heroes, Enos Slaughter, spiked Jackie in a play at first base, gashing his leg. Both teams were poised for a brawl, but Jackie just grabbed his ankle, looked, shrugged it off, and stayed in the game. I said, "Wow." On that day, I felt like the luckiest kid in the world, and to *this* day, few things have thrilled me as much as seeing Jackie Robinson play in his first season. The Brooklyn fans showed me how much they appreciated him.

Still, the experience was sobering. We had just finished a war that was supposedly pitting the forces of democracy against the forces of suppression of individual liberties. Yet African Americans, who had fought and died—as they had in all American wars—returned to the United States and were summarily denied human rights.

The summer after I graduated high school, I got a job running an elevator in a downtown office building. Standing at my post, I noticed how many young people were getting on the elevator to work in the offices—an option that wasn't available to me. I became friendly with a white guy my age, and I asked him if he'd just graduated. He said yes. "Me, too," I said. "What are you doing?" He described his job working in the office, and I said, "I could do those things." We struck up a good friendship, but I was painfully aware that the competition was fixed in my case.

CHAPTER TWO

Sergeant Wilder

I WAS IN A HURRY TO GET ON WITH MY LIFE, AND I GRADUATED FROM high school at age sixteen. I wanted to go into the navy. I didn't have money or connections to get into college. But my parents refused to sign for me. So I enrolled as a biology major at Virginia Union University, an African American college in Richmond, and worked to earn my own way. My choice of a major was not based on anything more than the idea that the "smart boys" pursued medicine as a profession, and biology was the first step. After a year, I changed my major to chemistry because I didn't like my biology teacher. We didn't have high school counselors, and Virginia Union didn't have the resources for counseling either, so I was on my own to figure out my path. Needless to say, chemistry and I did not get along that well, although I subsequently worked for a while as a chemical lab technician before entering law school.

The tuition for college was $150, and there was a $50 scholarship if you maintained a C average for each semester. In short, for $200 a year or less, you could get a college education. That's what Virginia Union was committed to. This school was founded from Lumpkin's Jail, located in Richmond's Shockoe Bottom, where "Negroes" were first exposed to learning. I'd inevitably be in line for late registration after I scraped the money together. "You again, Wilder?" the registrar would ask, amused.

I earned money by waiting tables at hotels where political events were common. I would hang back and listen to the speeches and found that my political education was evolving. In their midst, I felt invisible. I'd read Ralph Ellison's *Invisible Man*, and in that setting, I understood what he meant. As I was serving coffee and pouring tea, the men would be telling racist jokes right in front of me. That made an impression on me. I was angry, but I had been taught not to react in anger but to strive to be better.

To this day, I recall the time Robert Taft, who was running for president, spoke at a luncheon of white supporters at the William Byrd Hotel before coming over to speak to African American students at Virginia Union. Taft was a conservative Republican from Ohio who often aligned himself with conservative southern Democrats. Taft opposed the New Deal and the American engagement in World War II. Although he was of a different party, he was a big supporter of Harry Byrd and openly stated that he admired his principles, especially states' rights, the code for segregation.

At the William Byrd, Taft offered the crowd what it wanted to hear— what amounted to red meat for the segregationists. At Virginia Union, he gave an opposite speech, telling us how devoted he was to the cause of equality and opportunity for our people. I couldn't believe the bald-faced pandering—lying!—and it outraged me. I was further outraged that the organizer of the event at Virginia Union, a professor who subsequently became a good friend of mine, refused to recognize me so that I could point out this discrepancy. He also would not recognize a good friend of mine who was working at the hotel with me. Perhaps that was my awakening to engagement, but I didn't yet see what my role would be. Few of my classmates were disturbed or exercised about inequality, but I could not reconcile with even tacit acquiescence.

I had been made to learn and appreciate that "the price of ignorance is brutality." The admonition of Socrates likewise hovered in my mind: "Know you're right, then proceed." I was determined to learn as much as I could about why I had to live as a lesser person and what I could do about it.

In college, I was a restless student, hungry for knowledge. I wanted to know about everything, not just the subjects of my classes. If I was in chemistry class, I'd distract the professor with a diversionary discussion about world events. In ethics class, I'd talk about race. I would frequently change the discussion in my classes because I wanted to understand on a deeper level what education was all about and what it meant to me. I craved the opportunity to be heard, especially living in a nation where *we* were not heard. I had ambitions for myself beyond the stifling confines of segregation, and on some level, I realized that if change were to come, it had to start within my own heart. I couldn't be a bystander. I had to plow new ground or watch the weeds grow.

But when I graduated in 1951 with a degree in chemistry, the world was not open to me. I went to the state employment agency, looking for work. "What do you do?" the man asked me.

"I have a degree in chemistry," I said proudly.

He looked me over. "I don't have anything like that. But I do have a job you might be interested in. We need a cook over at the Hanover School for Boys."

I stared at him uncomprehendingly. "I don't know anything about cooking," I said.

"You'll learn."

I remember feeling humiliated by the experience, and I said no thanks. The memory stayed with me of how it felt to be put down that way. Many years later, as governor, I'd walk through the gates of the governor's mansion, which was adjacent to the old building housing the Employment Office, and smile and say to myself, "I think I've been able to find a job."

My postcollege job search did not last long because the Korean War was upon us. I was drafted in March 1952 and sent to Fort Meade in Maryland and then on to Camp Breckinridge in Kentucky for sixteen weeks of basic training.

Camp Breckinridge was hot, dusty, and hilly—excellent preparation for Korea. It was a vast army post on 36,000 acres, named after John C. Breckinridge, who had been the vice president of the United States under James Buchanan and then the secretary of war for the Confederacy. During World War II, Camp Breckinridge was used to house several thousand German prisoners of war, and it was brought back into use as an infantry training camp for the Korean War.

President Truman had integrated the army by executive order, so it was my first experience not only living with white Americans but also interacting with them in a meaningful way. During four months of training, I learned the operation of every weapon I would use in Korea—carbine and M-1 rifles and mortars. I made squad leader there, and I considered going to officer's training school, but ultimately I turned it down. It would have meant eighteen additional months of service.

My flight from Richmond to Seattle was another first. I had never been on a plane before. In Seattle, I boarded the USS *Collins*, along with three thousand other men, for a trip across the ocean to the city of Yokohama in Japan. From there, we'd go to Korea. A buddy of mine, William C. Watson, was on the ship with me. He had served in the Merchant Marine, and he was invaluable in helping me overcome seasickness during our rocky journey.

At Camp Breckinridge, I'd sung with a jazz band that used to perform out in the community, and I sang with a band aboard the ship. Someone advised me that my ability could get me into special services and I could apply. I rejected the idea. I also rejected the idea of using my chemistry degree to apply for a post in chemical warfare. Those positions might not have been on the front lines, but they came with the extra eighteen-month service time. My goal was to get in and out in nine months. I ended up staying thirteen months, with ten of them on the front lines.

We traveled to Tokyo in September, then on to Korea. I was in the 7th Division, 17th Infantry Regiment, 1st Battalion. When I arrived at the front, all was quiet. I ran into a friend coming in from the demilitarized zone (DMZ). He was heading home. Everything was calm, he told me. There was nothing going on. I even wrote my mother that it was a piece of cake.

Then, on October 6, all hell broke loose. The Chinese launched what was equivalent to the Tet Offensive in Vietnam all along the DMZ. The Chinese took most of the highest hills, and their goal was to wipe out our trenches and communication systems below. I went back and told the company commander, "I've changed my mind. I think I'd like that chemical warfare slot." He laughed. "I guess you would," he said. "I'm trying to get out of here, too. Wilder, you're stuck here."

Suddenly, my world was rocked by death and injury all around me. There was a guy named Skinner who was a real madcap. Skinner liked to taunt the enemy. The fighting occurred mostly at night, and during the day, we rested and regrouped in hoochies, shelters that were half aboveground and half below, buttressed by sandbags. Skinner, however, would go out every morning and take potshots at the Chinese. He enjoyed it. It was fun for him—until they fired back.

One morning, I heard firing and ran out to see what was going on. I encountered the most horrifying sight of my life—one that still haunts me. What I saw was a headless body jumping around, the nerves still active. It was running in circles before finally collapsing. Skinner. The Chinese had finally responded to his taunt. For the next few days, I was rattled. It took me a while to get over it. The next time I wrote to my mother, I lied to her when I said everything was calm.

In the army, I learned how to lead and how to follow. I went from being a relatively undisciplined young man to a disciplined adult. To this day, my children marvel at my pristine housekeeping and ask if I'm expecting company. "Yes," I tell them, "me." The army taught me to respect myself and others, and the lesson never left me.

In Korea, in the newly integrated army, the commanders seemed to take the notion of equality to heart. When we first arrived, Major Earl C. Acuff pulled us together and told us that we were going to be respectful of one another. He didn't want to hear about any problems with race. Our job was to fight a common foe. He told us if we had problems to come and see him.

Well, our relationships were good. No problems there. But as the weeks went by, we noticed that something else was going on. Time and again, we saw white men get promoted, even those who had been there for less time than we had. But no African Americans and no Hispanics were promoted. One day, an African American sergeant named Richburg pulled me aside. "This doesn't make any sense," he grumbled. "I should be master sergeant, but these others are getting promoted before me. It's like I'm invisible." He gave me a challenging look. "Didn't the major tell us about how we were all equal in the eyes of the army?"

"Yes," I said. "He certainly did."

"Do you think he meant it?"

"Yes, I think he did."

"Well, when are we going to see it?"

I said, "Look, the major will be back from the line tomorrow to take a shower." Once a month, they would let us go back to take a shower off the line. I suggested we go see the major, but first we should talk to the guys and find out their complaints.

We got all the African Americans together, and they had complaint after complaint after complaint. I said, "This is good." Richburg said, "Why don't we get everybody lined up, and you can march them on down."

I said, "I can't march these people. I'm a corporal. You're a sergeant. I don't mind getting them together, but you march them down." He said, "All right, but if we go, we're going to put on two bandoliers of ammunition on each side. Steel pots for our helmets. Our grenades put in our belts. Our sidearms and our M-1 rifles. Full dress."

I went to get the guys. "Before we go, we're going to take showers."

They weren't enthusiastic—"Shower, hell, man."

I insisted. I had to literally threaten them. "You're going to get up and take a shower, or I'm going to take this bayonet and stick you in your butt."

I got them all cleaned up and lined up, and we marched down to see the major. I can only imagine what people thought, seeing a group of twenty-five African Americans, all done up in their gear, marching past. We looked like a platoon. We had to follow the chain of command, so we needed permission from the first sergeant, then the company commander. The commander looked at us, all fixed up like our own platoon, and he asked, "What's this about?"

"Personal," I said. If you said it was personal, they had to let you through. They brought us in to see Acuff.

Acuff was taciturn and disciplined. He stood coolly, waiting for us to explain ourselves. I said, "Go ahead, guys, tell him about your experience." But suddenly everyone was too shy to speak, so I stepped forward and began to make our case.

Once I started, their tongues loosened, and the others took over. Acuff listened carefully, not cutting anyone off. Finally, Richburg said, "All of us thought our purpose in coming here was to unite to fight the common foe. We don't want to have to fight with our people here. We want to fight the North Koreans and the Chinese. That's what you told us."

Acuff said, "Yes, I do recall what I told you. Here's what I want you to do. Go back to your units, do your jobs, keep your word, and you'll see that I'll keep mine." Sure as hell, the next month, there were promotions, and in the months following, there were more. I made staff sergeant and then tech sergeant. I learned that there are decent people who would do the right thing. Acuff could have fed us a line and done nothing, but he acted.

I didn't realize it at the time, but my involvement in this matter was sowing the seeds of a future legal career. I became very concerned with those needing representation. I saw that people were not always able or willing to describe what had happened to them, that someone had to step out in front and argue their case. Before I knew it, the idea was settling inside of me that this is what I wanted to do. I knew that once I returned to Virginia, I couldn't live the same life.

Now, when guys had problems, they came to me, and I'd help them if I could. I remember one soldier who fell asleep on guard duty and was facing court-martial. He asked me to represent him. It turned out that during the time we were waiting for trial, he distinguished himself in action and was put in for the Silver Star. I urged the military to drop the court-martial, and it did. How could you simultaneously court-martial a man while awarding him the Silver Star?

Most of my time in Korea was spent in the center of battle, on Old Baldy and Pork Chop Hill. Many countries sent units to support us—Greeks, Australians, Brits, Canadians, French, and Colombians. The best ground fighters of all were the Ethiopians. They trained in Ethiopia at night and in hilly and mountainous terrain, so they were accustomed to the mountains and the dark. If I knew that the Ethiopians were either to my left or to my right, I relaxed a little. I also felt comfortably flanked by the first Marine Corps.

Often I found myself at listening posts, which were outposts of the main line of resistance. We'd stay there from sundown to sunrise, listening and reporting. One night, four of us were at the listening post when a mortar barrage came at us. One guy was killed instantly, and another was lying on the side of the hill with internal injuries. I reached over to the third man's arm and grabbed a stump. His arm was gone. I didn't have a scratch.

In war, the difference between life and death can be an inch or a moment. You have to try not to dwell on the ever-present danger, the horror you've experienced, or the possibility that in an instant your number could be up. I had a good friend named Jim Cunningham, a graduate of the University of Southern California who worked in phone communications. His job was to repair the lines if they were blown up by mortar shells. He'd come by my hoochie, and we'd have long conversations about history and philosophy and our lives. One day, he came by and said, "You got a break?" I did, and he suggested I accompany him while he repaired damaged communication lines. We walked and talked, and as we neared the hoochie, we noticed a change in the air. It got real quiet. That's what happens just before a mortar hit. You couldn't hear it. Suddenly Jim pushed me and yelled, "Move!" I fell to the ground with Jim on top of me and felt the percussion of the mortar shell. After a few moments, I pushed at Jim, who was half draped over me. "We can get up now." Then I saw his face, which was turning white. He said, "I'm done for," and he died. He saved my life and lost his own. Stunned, I crawled over to a corner and put my head down as the medics rushed forward. I couldn't bring myself to acknowledge that Jim was dead. Except for his quick action, it would have been me.

Another time, a friend, W. C. "Bill" Watson, came by my hoochie. "I got a package from home," he said. "I know some cake's in it. Come on over and get some." I went over and shared his goods, and when I returned, I found that my hoochie had been obliterated. That's where I would have been if I hadn't been eating cake.

Toward the end of my rotation, the fighting was fierce on Pork Chop Hill. I had no idea that the Chinese had taken it; we thought there were only three or four of them up there. There were three of us going up the hill—me, a guy named Wyatt, and a Korean attached to the army named Koo. Koo and Wyatt were inseparable. They spent their spare time teaching each other their languages.

As we were going up the hill, we heard a burp gun coming from a hoochie ahead of us. Wyatt was a gung-ho guy. Totally fearless. He said, "You cover the opening. Koo and I will go around back to put a thermite grenade in the sandbags, and when the guy comes out, you take him."

Koo ran forward and immediately got shot down. He died instantly. Wyatt kept going and planted the grenade. But instead of one guy coming out of the hoochie, there were twenty guys. Wyatt and I looked at each other in horror, realizing that if those twenty men knew there were only two of us, we'd be sunk.

"We've got to act like there are more of us," I said quietly, and then shouted, "We got 'em! All right, men!" Thankfully, it was pitch black, and we were able to bring off the ruse.

I called, by sound power, to the command post at the bottom of the hill and said that we were bringing twenty prisoners down. "We've got to be a little careful," I whispered. "There's only two of us."

We lined up the prisoners, and it took a good thirty minutes to get to the bottom. There was a new lieutenant on duty. He'd been there only two weeks, and his inexperience showed. One night, I was out with him, and he turned on a flashlight, an inexcusably stupid move.

The lieutenant said, "Good job, Wilder." I told him, "Wyatt's the guy who came up with the strategy. He was the hero. I want to put Wyatt in for the Silver Star."

"I'll take care of it," he said.

"Make sure you do," I said. "Without what Wyatt did, we wouldn't be here. He deserves the Silver Star."

"I got it," he said.

"W-Y-A-T-T," I spelled, just for good measure.

I finally rotated out in August 1953, having received my discharge paperwork the day before the armistice, and went back to Fort Meade, Maryland. I was ordered to be available for division review, which involved about 15,000 troops. Shortly beforehand, I received a notice that I was being awarded the Bronze Star for capturing those prisoners. I didn't see Wyatt's name anywhere. That agitated me. Then I saw with disgust that the new lieutenant had put himself in for the Silver Star. He didn't do anything but receive the prisoners Wyatt captured. He stole Wyatt's Silver Star. From then on, whenever I saw people getting medals, I always thought of the many others who deserved them and were passed over. Those great soldiers, better than me, better than most of us, were left unrewarded, and it hurt me to think about it. Since that experience, I always told people, "Don't tell me how brave you are because of the medals you got."

I also contemplated the vast separation between the generals and the fighting men. Generals send soldiers to fight, but for them, war can be an abstract calculation. You don't see generals on the front. I remember one time when some of the generals at the Pentagon decided they were going to view the fighting forces during an operation called Operation Smack. Our goal was to take over a hill called Spud Hill. Behind Spud at the main line, they constructed a concrete bunker to serve as a viewing station for the generals. The attack was unsuccessful, and a reporter from *Stars and Stripes* caused an uproar when he wrote that Operation Smack was just a publicity stunt for the brass. Whether or not that was true, it was a sobering experience. In later years, when I visited veterans' hospitals and witnessed so many broken lives, I concluded that if you're going to ask someone to die or be wounded for their country, it better be worth it.

When I got back home, I never talked about my Bronze Star because what happened to Wyatt cheapened the whole thing for me. I put a certificate on the wall of my office and left it at that. In 1985, when I was running for lieutenant governor, my campaign manager, Paul Goldman, saw the certificate on my wall. "We have to use this," he insisted. I was reluctant, but he convinced me to let him publish a picture of the award with the slogan "From Korea to the U.S.A.—Still Fighting for Virginia."

To my amazement, a group of Asians in Northern Virginia protested the ad. They accused me of using a racial appeal by speaking against Koreans. Since this was nearly the only time I'd openly talked about my service or my Bronze Star, I was shocked by the response. I hardly knew what to say. Surely, I had not meant to offend a whole community of people. Had we not been fighting *for* the Koreans in the war? Before I had a chance to figure out a response, two powerhouses of the opposing party—Virginia Senator John Warner, a Korean War navy veteran, and New Hampshire Senator Warren Rudman—stuck up for me and publicly chastised the Asian community for questioning my intentions. My own party wouldn't touch the issue, but those two Republicans gave them hell. I never forgot it.

The Korean War was a hellish experience. It took me ten years to stop having nightmares. I relived the experience in my dreams, and in dreams, you can't run. Trapped in a hole, the Chinese coming to get me, I'd cry out. My mother knew enough to wake me up, and then my wife did too. Eventually, I stopped having nightmares. But to this day, the sound of an unexpected explosion causes me to jump. It's a conditioned response, the lasting legacy of being in battle. The Korean War made a man out of me, but no one leaves the battlefield completely whole.

CHAPTER THREE

The Home Trenches

RETURNING HOME FROM THE WAR WAS BITTERSWEET. I WAS ALIVE, BUT the truth of my circumstances became depressingly clear. I had been called to fight for the freedom of a people when I did not have that same freedom. I could not sit where I wanted to sit, eat where I wanted to eat, or walk where I wanted to walk. The doors of America's greatest institutions were closed to me. A majority of my fellow Virginians considered me less than human—or at least less than equal. I was awarded the Bronze Star, but I was very uncertain of my place in society.

I might have become bitter, but in 1954, months after my return, something extraordinary occurred. Nine white men on the Supreme Court of the United States unanimously ended school segregation with a ruling in *Brown v. Board of Education*. That decision restored my faith in America and lifted my spirits. I saw the door creaking open, and I knew that America was, as Theodore White said, "still in search of itself." The *Brown* decision meant everything to me, and it turned my life around because that's when I decided to pursue a career in law. I wanted to be a part of this marvelous social engineering. I strongly believed that if African Americans had full access to education, there was nothing they couldn't achieve. The key to achieving equality was education.

Before *Brown*, there was always a sentiment lingering in the air around us: "What more do you want?" We had been delivered from slavery, and abolitionist efforts provided a modicum of security. Especially in Virginia, outward behavior toward African Americans was unfailingly polite. But the reality was an apartheid that kept us in our place. Into this uneasy cohabitation, the Supreme Court ruling desegregating schools was a nuclear shock to the system. And Virginia fought back.

In Virginia, where the Byrd organization held sway, attacking integration was a grand mission, and the *Brown* decision caused an explosive reaction. On May 17, 1954, after the decision in *Brown* was announced, Byrd issued an immediate statement to the press that showed he was gearing up for a fight: "The unanimous decision of the Supreme Court to abolish segregation in public education is not only sweeping but will bring implications and dangers of the greatest consequence. It is the most serious blow that has yet been struck against the rights of the states in a matter vitally affecting their authority and welfare. . . . The decision will be deplored by millions of Americans, and, instead of promoting the education of our children, it is my belief that it will have the opposite effect in many areas of the country. In Virginia we are facing now a crisis of the first magnitude."

Byrd's first step was a stalling action. He enlisted the political infrastructure, led by Governor Thomas Bahnson Stanley, in the fight to maintain the status quo. African Americans in Virginia would have to wait for equality while the governor appointed a commission to study how the state might resist the ruling. In fairness to Stanley, he was a somewhat reluctant recruit to Byrd's cause. His first reaction was to say, in effect, let's take this slowly and not act precipitously. That mild-mannered response did not sit well with Byrd, who had the weight to pressure Stanley. In the end, the commission that Stanley appointed was stacked against integration—comprised of thirty-two white male state legislators, representing the most conservative corners of the state. It was chaired by Garland Gray, an outspoken segregationist, whose fighting words rang throughout the land that "no child be required to attend an integrated school." The commission took a year to come up with its proposal, and the result was predictable:

- Laws concerning school attendance should be amended so that no child would be required to attend an integrated school.

- Funds should be allocated as tuition grants for parents who opposed schools comprised of white and black students.

- Local school boards should be authorized to assign white and black students to particular schools.

Perhaps unsurprisingly the commission's proposal was not strong enough to appease Byrd, who stated with a firebrand's fervor, "If we can organize the Southern States for massive resistance to this order, I think that in time the rest of the country will realize that racial integration is not going to be accepted in the South." Byrd urged his fellow politicians to sign the "Southern Manifesto" opposing the Supreme Court decision, and one hundred of them joined him. In this way, my home state became a leader of the fight to oppose school integration. "Massive resistance" became codified in state law. It captured the Virginia mood not only about race but also its inherent distaste for being told what to do by the federal government. In 1956, the state assembly adopted a resolution "to resist this illegal encroachment upon our sovereign powers, and to urge upon our sister states, whose authority over their own most cherished powers may next be imperiled, their prompt and deliberate effort to check this and further encroachment by the Supreme Court, through judicial legislation, upon the reserved powers of the states."

Many would say this was strictly a states' rights battle, a response to federal overreach. That might have been true in the same way that the Civil War was a states' rights battle. But the essence of the battle, its reason for being, was race, pure and simple. I cannot think of another matter that so stirred the hearts of southerners toward resistance.

Some of the resistance efforts would have been comical if they hadn't been so tragic. For example, a Pupil Placement Board was established for district school boards to refer black applicants to white schools. Make no mistake—its purpose was resistance. If a poor, trusting student submitted an application—and it was difficult to even procure an application form—it would be whisked away to the board, which would then issue a denial. If the student then disputed the rejection in federal court (and, face it, how many would do that?), it would begin a very lengthy and probably expensive legal runaround. In fact, without direct federal intervention, the state wielded enormous power to make integration impossible.

But as Martin Luther King Jr. would observe, "The arc of the moral universe is long but it bends toward justice." Efforts to halt integration in Virginia schools collapsed in 1959, five years after the *Brown* decision. After schools were closed in Prince Edward, Norfolk, and Warren counties rather than integrating, the Virginia Supreme Court finally ruled that any law prohibiting integrated public schools was unconstitutional. The Byrd organization had overplayed its hand. It turned out that while the public might have supported massive resistance in principle, they didn't want schools closed. They didn't want chaos. They didn't want to be stuck on a train heading into the last century. In particular, there was a growing drumbeat from the business community, which was concerned that massive resistance would undermine economic development. School segregation was a lost cause, and everybody knew it. By the time the Virginia Supreme Court ruled, most people were just relieved, although it didn't mean the fight was completely over. There were many layers of controversy that had to be unraveled. In the 1970s, the conflicts over busing threatened the entire system, causing annexations, white flight, and tangentially the deterioration of the inner cities. Many of those issues continue to this day through debates about quotas and districting. Yet having said all that, I will never forget the joy in my heart when those nine justices put a stake through the heart of school segregation.

While the possibility enshrined in the *Brown* decision raised my hopes, the realities on the ground were still difficult. In 1956, when I decided to use the GI Bill to go to law school, my ambition was high, but my options were limited. White law schools in Virginia were closed to me, and I was accepted at Howard University in Washington, the nation's first African American law school. I entered, determined to become a leading lawyer back in Church Hill. My roommate was Henry Marsh, who would later distinguish himself as a prominent civil rights attorney and the first African American mayor of Richmond—not elected but selected by the city council, which at the time included five blacks and four whites.

Another of my classmates was a friend named Bruce Boynton from Montgomery, Alabama. During a school break, Bruce was returning home to Alabama on a Trailways bus, and there was a forty-minute stop-over at the Stay Away Trailways Bus Station in Richmond. Waiting in that station, Bruce sat down at the lunch counter in the whites-only section of the station's restaurant and was arrested. Bruce tried to call me, but I wasn't in, so he called Henry Marsh, who set him up with Oliver Hill and Samuel Tucker, local African American lawyers who were involved in many civil rights cases, including the *Brown* decision. They took the case and worked with the NAACP under the leadership of Thurgood Marshall. In *Boynton v. Virginia*, Marshall argued that Bruce had been denied equal protection under the law. In a seven-to-two decision, the Supreme Court ruled that all passengers were protected by the Interstate Commerce Act, and the facilities in bus stations were considered part of interstate commerce.

I was proud of Bruce, but not everyone understood why he did what he did. Even some of our own folks wondered. I told them, "He just decided enough was enough." That sense of coming to the end of the line was being experienced across the South in the early 1960s. It would be a decade of African Americans standing their ground.

By the time I graduated from law school in 1959, I was married and soon to be a father. African Americans were not allowed to belong to the bar association. In fact, there was a quota where only one African American per year could pass the bar. But it was virtually impossible to even take the exam. I couldn't take the bar review course at the

University of Richmond because it was segregated. I was on my own. Dudley Woodbridge, former dean of the Law School at William & Mary, compiled a study course known as Woodbridge's Notes, which sold for $10 or $15. I sent for a copy. It was a well-documented and a thorough review of all of the previous questions and answers to several years of bar examinations.

While I was waiting to take the bar exam, I got an offer from Hale Thompson, an African American lawyer in Newport News, to work in his office. It was about an hour away from Richmond. I settled my family in my parents' home and found a room about fifteen blocks from Thompson's office. My pay was $35 a week. I had sold my car and rode the bus from Richmond to Newport News and came home on the weekends.

I worked hard for Hale, and I learned how a law office should operate. But after a few months, I told him I was leaving to study for the bar exam. He said, "Well, don't expect to pass it the first time." I replied that I intended to do just that. He said, "If you pass it, I'll give you a set of the Virginia Code."

For the next three months, I holed up and studied, with only an occasional foray to the pool hall to clear my head. I passed the bar in 1959 on the first try, and I was the only African American candidate to pass that year. When I reminded Hale about the bet and the Virginia Code, he said he meant "if you were going to work for me." But I had already decided that I wanted to start my own practice.

Confident (and perhaps overconfident) about my prospects, I announced to my parents that we were moving out of their house and that I was setting up a law office three blocks away. Our first child, Lynn, was born that year, and I had to scramble to support my family. In the early days, I'd do just about anything, even traveling outside Richmond to handle small traffic cases for a few bucks. I was determined to get my name out there.

I kept my office open on Saturdays so the workers could see me on their days off. On many occasions, clients would arrive to find me dressed in work clothes cleaning the office. Not realizing I was the lawyer, they'd ask for him, and I'd say, "He'll be right with you." Then I'd go in the back, change my clothes, and return in my official role. No one was ever put off by my quick change. Some were even impressed that I didn't set myself above them.

Mr. Roane, who had been a sexton at St. John's Church when I was a boy, became my client. He had regularly come by our house, and he always gave me a nickel. My mother, suspicious that I was timing his walk so as to be present to receive my nickel, threatened to give me a thrashing if I was "begging." Now Mr. Roane came to my office, and I helped him draw up a deed to a property he was buying. He always paid cash. He wore high-top shoes and never owned a car. When he asked me to write his will, I discovered that he owned more than twenty properties outright. His salary was meager, but the tips were constant.

When I first started the practice of law, everything was segregated—the courtrooms, the jails, and the bar association. There was not a single African American judge sitting full-time in any court in Virginia. That lasted for many years until I was in the state senate.

I wasn't an activist in the civil rights movement, but I strongly believed I could make my contribution in various ways, chiefly by representing African American folks in the courts. Before long, I had a thriving practice. My reputation was earned by being a damn good trial lawyer.

There weren't many African American lawyers in Richmond at the time. There was the firm of Hill, Martin, and Robinson, which represented Boynton. There was Spottswood Robinson, who left the firm of Hill, Martin, and Robinson. I was a great admirer of Spott, who, along with Hill, had been instrumental in the *Brown* decision and was Thurgood Marshall's right-hand man. His father had been a friend of my father for many years. To look at him, you'd think Spott was white, with his straight black hair slicked back and his narrow face. He was a huge presence in our lives.

One day, Spott contacted me. "I understand you've opened up a law office," he said.

"I have."

"Well, I'd be very interested in talking with you."

I was a bit starstruck by a request from the great Spottswood Robinson. He explained that he didn't have room in his office but wondered if I could do work for him out of mine. I was glad to oblige. Spott sent me cases, and he also taught me a level of rigor and precision in the law that I hadn't encountered before. He was a taskmaster. For example, he'd ask me to write a letter to a judge, and I thought I was a pretty good communicator, and I'd write the letter. He'd read it and say, "That's not too bad." Then he'd strike out a word here and a word there and give it back to me. I'd try again, and this would go on for a few hours until he was satisfied. By that point, I was ready to kill him, but he was right.

Spott was the registered agent for the NAACP Legal Defense Fund, and one day in 1960, he called me. "I've got some news. They want me to be the dean at the Howard University School of Law. What do you think about it?"

I said, "It's bad news for me. Good news for you. You should take it."

"Yes," he said. "I will, and I'm going to tell Thurgood that I want you to replace me as the registered agent for the NAACP."

I was taken aback. "Thank you for that," I said cautiously, "but would he appoint me?"

He cut me off. "We've got some cases to try next week, and Thurgood's coming down. I want you to be there."

"Yes sir." There was no argument about it.

The next week, I walked into the restaurant where Thurgood was seated. He looked me over with a probing gaze and said, "Spott tells me that he wants you to take his place."

"Yes sir."

"It's done," he said briskly. "Sit down. Let's have lunch."

Being the registered agent for the NAACP Inc. Fund, as it later became known, meant that any cases involving the NAACP in Virginia had to be handled through me if they involved money. My role allowed me to be tangentially involved in some of the great civil rights cases of the day. I saw that it mattered. As Thurgood put it, "The legal system can force open doors and sometimes even knock down walls, but it cannot build bridges. That job belongs to you and me."

It was a great experience for a young lawyer. I got to meet civil rights lawyers from all over the country. It was an honor just to be in a room with those guys! There was Ernest Nathan (Dutch) Morial from Louisiana, who would later become mayor of New Orleans; A. P. Trudeau, also from New Orleans; William Robert (Bob) Ming from Chicago, who had been on the *Brown* team; and, of course, the civil rights litigation giants of my own town—Oliver Hill and Samuel Tucker. These were brilliant lawyers, most of them working pro bono for the cause. Witnessing their commitment reinforced my own. I recognized that making a living was one thing, but I also had a role to play in representing those who were in danger of being left outside the system of justice unless I helped them. And in the process of standing up for others, I made a point of standing up for myself. I refused to sit in the "colored" section of the courtroom. The first time I sat at the white table, I expected an uproar, but no one said a word. From then on, I always sat at the white table. I also led the fight to open the bar association to African Americans. In my view, our system of justice was stained by segregation. True justice meant that the legal community would be open to all.

So, too, with representation. Chances were, if someone in Church Hill or anywhere in our community needed a lawyer, he or she came to me. (There were upwards of 70,000 people in Church Hill, and I knew the majority of them by their first names.) For the most part, these cases were not about race per se, but race was often the underlying issue. For example, one of the most interesting and, in many respects, important cases of my career was *Tucker v. Lower*, a landmark brain-death case with a racial element. In 1968, issues related to brain death had not yet been litigated. The definition of brain death was murky, and the ethics of organ donation were not entirely clear. One day, I received a call from a man named William Tucker, who had a horrifying story to tell. His fifty-six-year-old brother Bruce had sustained brain injuries in an accident and was brought to the Medical College of Virginia. There, he received an emergency craniotomy for a subdural hematoma. As his condition deteriorated, surgeons at the hospital began looking at him as a possible candidate for a heart and kidney transplant to a patient already in the hospital. (They'd been searching for a candidate for some time.) They asked police to try to contact his family, but contact was never made. When doctors determined that Bruce was brain-dead, they pronounced him "unclaimed dead" and discontinued the respirator that was keeping him alive. Although Virginia law required a two-day waiting period before disposing of unclaimed bodies, the surgical team, under the direction of Dr. Richard Lower, went ahead with the transplant of Bruce's organs, making the assumption that Bruce was a derelict. The recipient, Joseph Klett, a retired white executive, received Tucker's heart and lived for seven days with the organ before also dying.

By the time William learned that his brother had been injured and arrived at the hospital to check on his condition, the transplant was completed. He was told that his brother had died but not the circumstances of his death. And he learned of the transplant only after the undertaker told him his brother's organs had been removed.

When I took the case to trial, the defining issue was what constitutes death. Bruce might have been brain-dead, but was he *dead*, considering that doctors had to remove him from a respirator to stop his heart—and they neglected to record the details of exactly how and when his heart stopped beating. The secondary issue was related to consent. Why had the transplant gone forward without a diligent effort to contact Bruce's relatives? His brother William was known in the community, and he had a shoe repair shop right down the street from the hospital. The racial component was also clear. Bruce's race and socioeconomic circumstances made him vulnerable for organ removal, demonstrated by the simple fact that doctors declared him derelict without making much of an effort to find his family.

In court, the judge clearly sided with the doctors, agreeing with their premise that brain death meant actual death. The jury, forced to decide complex medical and ethical facts, ultimately sided with the doctors. But the case had great repercussions. Prior to the *Tucker* trial, the predominant view of death was a cessation of all vital organs. Brain death had never been considered a definition of death. As a result, there are those who feel that we now may have a more tolerant view toward interminable prolongation of suffering, eliminating the false hopes when most signs of life are gone. Wasteful expenses, unrealistic expectations, and an unnecessary continuation of suffering are less likely. Even so, poor old Bruce Tucker and his brother William got a raw deal. But they rewrote a new definition of death for the nation.

<hr />

Some people dream of holding political office for as long as they can remember. I was not one of those people. I wanted to be successful, and I wanted to be engaged in public life, but I had no desire to beg endlessly for money and to continually ask for public approval. However, as my reputation grew, so too did my associations in the community and across the state, and I began to ease my way into political action.

I talked it over with my mother. She was a widow by this time. My father had died in 1966 as he approached his eightieth birthday. He had smoked considerably in his lifetime—cigars, cigarettes, and even pipes—and he contracted lung cancer. Toward the end, he knew he was dying, and he did not want to stay in the hospital. He became unruly, and the doctor doubted that he could keep him there. My father put it to me straight: "Look, take me home; I don't need to die in here." So I lifted him up and put him in a wheelchair and brought him home. At home, he was very quiet, and he didn't go out much, although he insisted on attending church. He died in his own bed, which is what he wanted.

My law office was three blocks from our family home. I'd go to court in the morning and then drop by the house for breakfast. One day, I sat at the kitchen table and told my mother that I was considering going into politics. Her only question was, "Do you want to do this? Is it what you really want?"

"Yes," I said.

"Okay, then."

My mother was still my sharpest adviser and sometimes critic. She wasn't always so satisfied with the messy business of my law practice. On one occasion when I was defending a rapist, she shook her head soberly and said, "Oh, my God, is that what you went to law school for?" She'd make me explain myself.

Now she wondered if political office would negatively affect my law practice. I didn't think so, but I didn't really know. "Well," she said, "just don't get too carried away." My mother was always looking out for my ego! She was also concerned that my plans might interfere with spending time with my family, and I reassured her about that too. Although again, I didn't know. The path I was considering was unfamiliar to me. I had no mentors who could take me by the hand and advise me. I felt very much on my own. But I believed it was the right thing to do.

I knew it was time for African Americans to start winning elections, but I was disenchanted with the organizations that were setting up and endorsing candidates. Our community didn't know its own mind. Case in point: A prominent lawyer and community leader named Clarence Newsome planned to run for city council. He came to me for help, and I was glad to give it. I liked Newsome, and I thought he'd be the perfect candidate. We still hadn't broken the color barrier in the city council, and the last African American to even run had been Oliver Hill in 1948.

But the African American organizations weren't sold on Newsome, although he was associated with Hill's law firm. They thought he was too outspoken. So while they endorsed him, they also endorsed eight other candidates. "You're killing him!" I cried in frustration. And I was right. He didn't even come close. He finished tenth in a contest where nine council members were elected.

A big part of the problem was that African Americans were organizing around solidarity to a ticket rather than focusing on the issues. I can remember having frequent arguments, when I would say, "Don't you think we ought to expose people to what the issues are and what they mean?" And they'd reply, "No, we need to maximize solidarity. We need to make certain that people vote the right ticket and that they trust us." This was a point of view that was catastrophic to the cause of justice and equality. It was paternalistic and demeaning. The leaders, who should have known better, were saying, in effect, that African American folks didn't need to be educated, they didn't need to understand the issues, they just needed to vote the "right" way—the way they were told. It made me heartsick.

I knew I had to do something, so I formed my own group, along with three friends, called Voter's Voice. Our mission was to educate voters; we weren't running for office ourselves. Within a year, two members of our group did decide to run for office, so Voter's Voice broke up, but the need for political education was ever present, and I devoted myself to that mission. It was always my philosophy to respect the public. Many candidates just assumed that African American voters were (as I wrote passionately to the *Richmond News Leader*) "hordes of dumb cattle going through the motions of exercising a constitutional guarantee rather than being seriously affected by their country's future." I wanted to change that notion—to show people that they had an actual stake in the political process.

One way or another, I saw that I had to be part of the political discussion, whether I liked politics or not. You can't ask for change if you're not willing to step up.

When I did start thinking about political office, I had to admit I knew little about the legislative process. I had never seen the legislative body in action. I had never discussed issues with legislators. But I knew one thing: The system can work if we work it. We couldn't sit back and say, "Let them run it." It was time to step up.

In the waning years of the Byrd organization's influence, there were signs that it was just a matter of time before African Americans gained clout. Byrd and his cohorts were on the wrong side of history; their cause was unsustainable. By the time poor health drove the aging Byrd from the U.S. Senate in 1965, his Jim Crow era was already effectively over. Byrd died in 1966 and was replaced in the Senate by his son, Harry Byrd Jr. According to the *Washington Post*, "From his earliest days, he emulated his father and his walk, his speech and his philosophy. He even has the apple-cheeked glow that bespeaks hours spent outdoors and marks him, not as just a chip off the old block, but as an extension of the original." But the old Byrd foothold was beginning to slip.

By 1967, I was noticing a new dynamic in the electorate. That year, a moderate white Democrat from Richmond named J. Sargeant Reynolds had won a seat in the Virginia Senate with heavy support from the African American community. To be fair, African Americans hadn't necessarily come out in force just for "Sarge." A young physician, Dr. William Ferguson Reid, had also won a seat in the House of Delegates with the help of Reynolds and his friends. Reid had lost two years earlier to T. Dix Sutton, a write-in candidate, primarily because the votes in the "Skipwith" precinct were lost, thus allowing Reid to be the Democratic primary winner. He ultimately lost to Sutton in the general election. Reynolds had been endorsed by Reid and the African American community, resulting in his winning a house seat. Reid and Reynolds teamed up and Reid became the first African American elected to the General Assembly since Reconstruction. William S. Thornton, a podiatrist, who was also the leader of the predominantly African American voting group, the Richmond Crusade for Voters, was also running that year. But Thornton's group did the same thing they'd done with my friend Newsome, endorsing both Thornton and Reynolds. Thornton lost his race, but the beneficiary of the large African American turnout was the moderate Reynolds. The African American vote put Sarge over the top. Contemplating the result, I made the judgment that if an African American candidate could get on the ballot, one-on-one, against a white candidate, the African American could win.

In 1969, when Sarge announced that he was running for lieutenant governor, I began to put out feelers about running in the special election to fill his senate seat. The first thing I did was pay a visit to Thornton. I told him that if he was running for the seat, I would defer to him, but he said he wasn't interested in another campaign. And so I jumped into the race before anyone else.

My friends were doubtful about my run. My law school classmate and roommate, Henry Marsh, never endorsed or supported me for any office that I am aware of, although I had endorsed his run for the city council. His younger brother enthusiastically supported my campaigns, sometimes saying, "I don't know what the trouble is with Henry." Henry's excuse was that he wanted Thornton to run again, though Thornton publicly and privately said he had no such intention. People told me that I was crazy and that, if elected—a very big if, in their opinion—I'd be the only African American in the senate. I'd be alone. Rather than discouraging me, that fact increased my motivation. I looked around and saw that many of my contemporaries had lost hope and needed a sign that it was possible to get an African American elected. That's why I threw my hat into the ring. I was thirty-eight years old.

I was running on the Democratic ticket, but I intended to be on the ballot whether or not I got the party's nomination. I had two white opponents: former Richmond mayor Morrill Crowe for the Republicans and outgoing lieutenant governor Fred Pollard for the Democrats. It was far from smooth sailing. I was not closely associated with the civil rights movement in town or the Crusade for Voters, and they wanted their own candidate. What I had going for me were my relationships in Richmond, which were long and deep. Everyone knew me from either my law practice or my family.

But my campaign was surprising to many African Americans—and not necessarily in a good way. Rather than running as "their guy," I had a different message: "I want to be a bridge between poor and wealthy, young and the old, and black and white," I announced. I let them know that I wasn't going to use race as a badge or as a barrier. When people slapped me on the back and cried, "We're going to make history," I told them, "History doesn't pay the bills. It doesn't make the tax burden lighter. It doesn't pave the roads." I made it clear through my words and actions that I was representing all the people, not just *my* people. And some didn't care for that. However, I was on the leading edge of a new era of African American political action. To be part of the solution, you had to be part of the system, not hollering from the outside. And for an African American to win election, he had to draw support from a healthy percentage of white voters.

From the outset, my campaign held some surprises for African American voters. My first controversial act was to throw my support behind a plan for the city of Richmond to annex a section of the white suburbs—as long as there was a plan in place to ensure African American representation. It made economic sense, and I won some support from the business community for my stance. I also received help from Reynolds and many of his supporters, those Republicans with a liberal (and pragmatic) bent who wanted to shake off the paralyzing stigma of the Old South.

Campaigning for office, I learned something about myself: I loved getting out among the people. I had always been sociable, but this was a new kind of sociability, a chance to engage people on both an intellectual and an emotional level. African Americans would enthusiastically pump my hand and urge me on. Whites, however, had to be courted. Often, as I chatted with them, I could see them thinking, "He's not so bad." I did not fit the stereotype of the angry radical that was such an object of fear. Although my race was plain as day, I was determined not to make my campaign about race. I wanted people to vote their interests, and it was my task to convince them that I best represented those interests.

I enjoyed "retail" politics, and I was good at it. I didn't have to pretend or try to become someone else. There was nothing I relished more than walking down the street, visiting shops and restaurants, and chatting with folks along the way. It got so I was hard-pressed to get out of a room once I'd entered. People had plenty to say, and they craved a voice. Whites were interested in the novelty of my race and African Americans in its promise.

On election day, I felt confident, but election night was a roller coaster. The results trickled in, up and down throughout the evening. I was in a hotel room with my family and friends, and everyone was biting their nails. I remained calm. As the hour grew late with no final count, I announced, "I'm going to sleep." And I did—to everyone's astonishment.

By the time I woke up, my great gamble had paid off: The grandson of slaves became the first African American elected to the state senate since Reconstruction. I got most of the African American vote and a healthy percentage of the white vote, which was the key to my victory. Crowe and Pollard split the remaining white vote, just as I'd forecasted. In the end, I received 48.4 percent, Crowe 31.5 percent, and Pollard 18.6 percent. As the *Times-Dispatch* noted in an editorial following the election, "It would be wrong to view Wilder's achievement simply as a victory of blacks over whites. For upon reflection, it will become apparent that the white electorate itself indirectly contributed to Wilder's success." Or maybe not so indirectly. I broke the stalemate and showed whites that they didn't have to be scared of an African American representative.

Ironically, the 1969 election of a Republican, Linwood Holton, as governor, who was more moderate than his Democratic opponent, shined a light on the changing faces of the parties. While the Byrd-influenced Democrats were still fighting integration, Holton made it clear that he was part of a new era. Shortly after he took office, concerned about the outcry against forced busing, he placed his own children in the Richmond public schools, which at the time were mostly African American.

Sensitive to the concerns of the public, I laid my cards on the table in my acceptance speech. "I am very conscious that my margin of victory is a plurality and that the bulk of my support came from black citizens," I said. "To these supporters I pledge to be a long-needed listening post and a vigorous spokesman for their special concerns and needs. However, the returns indicate that I also received a gratifying number of white votes. I particularly appreciate this support, and I look forward to the time when all men can run as candidates on their qualifications and not as a 'Negro' candidate or a 'white' candidate."

And then I went to the senate, and my first act was the episode over the state song. People thought I'd lost my mind. "We didn't elect him to talk about some damn song," one frustrated activist in my own community said. But the way I viewed it, just like when I was a kid at the barbershop, was that my role was to teach people about the issues—to illuminate the way things were and edge them toward the way things should be.

Public service is a tautology. It defines itself. It means *to serve the public*. Not yourself. It doesn't mean that you become enriched or have your name emblazoned on headlines. There are two words to describe the mission of politics: *do it*. Don't talk about it. Do it. It's beautiful to have a vision, but the real point is to get things done—even when you're not sure (because who's ever sure?) of what the outcome will be. Politics in practice is a form of reality testing. It's similar to the way elephants were used to test the strength of new bridges by setting one foot down to see if it would hold before putting the next foot down. I felt like those elephants, always testing the strength of the bridge.

Public service for me has never been about the glory of the office and getting elected. Nor was it about "giving back" because nothing had ever been given TO me. It means being a part of the decision making: What's going to go on? What role do I play in it? It's about making the impossible possible. All my life I heard, "Don't let anyone tell you that you can't do something." But it's not enough to get in the door; you've got to be smart, you've got to GOVERN. Likewise, the citizens have an obligation. When I went to a community, I always spoke about organizing. The message is, "Don't just tell me what you need, tell me what you're going to *do*." It's a collective effort. That's what democracy means.

After the state song controversy, some people started calling me a maverick, but I never saw myself that way. And I learned that the truth was found not in how people define you but in how you define yourself. If I'd seen myself as a maverick, it would have undermined my effectiveness. I chose instead to think of myself as a person who wanted what any reasonable person wanted—that is, the right thing. I'd say, "If the thing is right, the time is right to do it," and the line captured my philosophy in a nutshell.

That was all fine and good, but I was a novice in the senate. I had no idea how the place worked or what my actual role would be. I didn't even understand how committee assignments were doled out. The learning curve was steep, but I stuck to my pledge of being a bridge builder. There was racial pride associated with my election, but I never saw myself as just a representative of the African American community—as I'm sure many of my constituents did. I always looked first at the issues, and when I spoke about remedies, be they in education or health or housing or the justice system, I never focused on remedies for African Americans alone. The point was to provide remedies and opportunities for *all* the people.

My mother was proud of me, but as she had done my entire life, she didn't hesitate to keep me grounded. "Now, don't you go getting a swelled head," she'd say, and I'd laugh appreciatively, knowing there was no escape from her probing eye. She'd always let me know when she thought I was getting too big for my britches.

I don't think my mother ever expected to live into her eighties, but she did—conquering cervical cancer only to die at eighty-three of heart disease. She was visiting my sister in North Carolina when she became ill, and my sister called me to say the end was near. "Tell her I'm coming," I said and raced south to be by her side. When I arrived at the hospital, she was weak but still alive. I took her frail hand, and we spoke quietly for some time. She died that night. I've never stopped missing her, and my greatest regret is that she wasn't alive to see me sworn in as governor of Virginia in 1989. I can hear her voice as plain as day saying, "Now, don't you go getting a swelled head."

By the time I was elected to the senate, my law practice was thriving. The legislature in Virginia is part-time, and at first it took 20 percent of my time and then grew to more. They say that the law is a jealous mistress, and that's doubly true of politics. Eventually, I was spending upwards of 75 percent of my time on senate business.

I learned how to get things done and became an adept negotiator and an open-minded collaborator. I was always willing to work across the aisle and form relationships. But I never ducked a race-based challenge. On one occasion, I criticized a bill that would have given tax-exempt status to a country club in a wealthy Richmond neighborhood that denied entry to

African Americans and other minorities. In my remarks opposing the bill, I pointed out that one of the neighborhood's residents was Richmond native Willie Lanier, a famous linebacker for the Kansas City Chiefs (who would later be inducted into the Pro Football Hall of Fame). Lanier had applied for membership in the country club and been denied. I joked on the floor that perhaps it was Lanier's *height*—six feet one inch—that was the problem. Perhaps at 245 pounds, he was too *big* to play golf on their pristine greens. I never mentioned race, but my colleagues got the point, and the bill never advanced. Being an optimist, I believed that my colleagues in the senate wanted to do the right thing. Sometimes they needed a little help.

I never had any opponent oppose me during the sixteen years that I served in the senate. Consequently, I was pretty much regarded as a spokesperson on subjects pertaining to politics, government, and public affairs. My social calendar was full, and I confess to having enjoyed my place in the sun. My wife likewise was quite involved socially and highly regarded in the community.

My wife and I had three growing children—Lynn Diana, Lawrence Douglas Jr., and Loren Deane—and I struggled to find time for my family. By the mid-1970s, I could see that my marriage was crumbling. I have never discussed my divorce, and, in truth, divorce was anathema in my family. My mother would often tell us children, "Even if you make a bad bed, you still must lie in it." As odd as it may seem to some, my former wife and I never had any conversation about divorce. But we were struggling.

Six years after being elected to the Virginia State Senate, I had become a highly publicized political figure. Constant demand for appearances and speaking engagements throughout the state and beyond kept me furiously busy. I spent less time with my family and more time trying to keep my law practice and my political career going. I tried to make up for the time away from the law practice by working late at night, Saturdays and Sundays, and even some holidays.

I had bought a pony for my children, which they named Tonka. I still have pangs of guilt when I recall the plaintive pleas of my youngest daughter, Loren: "Dad, can we go out and see Tonka?"—and I would have to decline for some reason that on reflection was not more important.

By not taking the time to take the kids to go see their pony on the outskirts of town, I conveyed the message that what they wanted was not important. Even if my wife took them, she wasn't able to saddle up the pony or hitch him to the cart, and the kids were disappointed. At the time, I felt I didn't have a choice. I feel differently about that now.

After years going on this way, our marriage finally came to an end in 1978. The children were young—Lynn was fifteen, Larry thirteen, and Loren ten. I felt they should remain with their mother, and they did. We never argued over custody. My children grew into fine adults, and they have been by my side throughout my political career.

<hr/>

The ordinary business of the state fully engaged me, but if I were going to point to my proudest achievements in the senate, there would be two. The first was getting the first African American judges in Virginia elected by the legislature. Willard Douglas was named to Richmond's juvenile and domestic relations court in 1972 despite heavy opposition. Then James Sheffield was named to the Richmond circuit court. Phillip B. Morris, a member of the House of Delegates, was the leading force in getting the House Democratic Caucus to endorse Sheffield. Morris, who had been helpful in my election to the senate after his election to the House, said to me, "Doug, I did my part, now you do yours." I was able to get the senate Democratic caucus to endorse Sheffield over my senior colleagues' choice. Ed Willey, the most senior member of the senate, who chaired the Finance Committee, opposed me, but he became one of my closest friends and supporters in the senate thereafter. Sheffield was later nominated by President Carter to a federal judgeship, but he was blocked by Harry Byrd Jr. It's customary in the U.S. Senate for senators to give tacit approval—or disapproval—of judges nominated from their states. Byrd, in typical form, made the claim that this dignified, experienced, and well-regarded judge was unqualified. "I can't imagine anything worse for the American people than to have a quota system for federal judges," he said, thus ensuring that an African American federal judge from Virginia would not be seated on his watch. This claim of quota systems was a tool commonly used to prevent highly qualified African Americans, women, and other minorities from reaching positions of power and influence. It goes on to this day.

The second significant endeavor of my time in the senate was my effort to give Martin Luther King Jr. an official state holiday. It would turn into nearly a ten-year ordeal, beginning in 1975, and it wouldn't end until the year before I left the senate.

Virginia already had a notable state holiday—Lee-Jackson Day, which honored Confederate leaders Robert E. Lee and Thomas "Stonewall" Jackson. Our state began observing Lee's birthday way back in 1889, and Jackson was added in 1904. This holiday was celebrated on January 19, and it was sacrosanct. When I told my colleagues I was going to put a bill on the floor proposing a state holiday honoring Martin Luther King Jr., they couldn't believe it, especially when they saw that the language of my bill stipulated that King's name would be added to Lee-Jackson Day. People were apoplectic. The Daughters of the Confederacy and others screamed bloody murder, and one of the things they said was, "Any other day." They played right into my hands. "Okay," I said, and suggested January 15, King's birthday, which is what I'd had in mind from the outset. I outmaneuvered the detractors, and the bill passed the legislature, only to be vetoed twice by Governors Mills Godwin and John Dalton. I kept bringing the bill back. I was determined.

The drumbeat against the bill was fierce and steady. The media covered it, and I received piles of letters railing against King as a communist, a traitor, a philanderer, and so on. "How could we honor a traitor to our country with a state holiday?" the letter writers would demand while I contemplated the irony. Who were Lee and Jackson, if not traitors? But that was an argument that could not be made in Virginia, where these men were regarded as Confederate heroes. I recall receiving a brass coin with "nigger gold" engraved on one side and "coon coin" on the other during the debate.

I saw how much political courage it took for many of my colleagues to vote for the bill. It was embarrassing to some of the people who voted no. They'd apologize to me privately. They'd promise to support me behind the scenes. And I fully understood that their seats were on the line. But I assured them that the issue was not going away. Every time it was defeated, I brought it back the following year. If the senate passed it, the house would kill it. If it passed both houses, the governor would veto it. And I'd bring it back again.

In my years in the senate, I was always most concerned about enabling ordinary folks to achieve a level of clout. And that meant organizing. I could not abide people standing on the sidelines when the most important issues of the day were on our plate. In spite of my success politically, during my first decade in the senate, the indelible stamp of "the Organization" colored everything that happened in our state. But things were changing. To that end, I organized the Virginia Democratic Black Caucus. My good friend Dr. Calvin M. Miller, head of the Department of Political Science at Virginia State University, was instrumental in helping to form the group. I ultimately became chair of both the Democratic Black Caucus and the Legislative Black Caucus, even though the members on the latter were no more than three.

The Democratic Black Caucus drew its membership from across the state. I scheduled meetings for Saturday afternoons at Virginia Union University, my alma mater, and people traveled to be there. They came from the Tidewater area of Norfolk, Hampton, and Newport News. They came from the Northern Virginia areas of Alexandria, Arlington, Fairfax, Loudon, and Prince William. They came from the Northern Neck area of Gloucester, Isle of Wight, Tappahannock, and even as far west as Montgomery, Christiansburg, and Roanoke. They came from the central areas of the state—Harrisonburg, Orange, and Culpeper counties.

In those rousing sessions, I sensed a hunger for participation, a desire to be engaged. For the attendees, joining the Democratic Black Caucus meant having a seat at the table for the first time. I remember people marveling on many occasions that no one had ever asked their opinions before or told them they could hold political sway in elections. It was liberating and energizing.

Naturally, the Democratic Black Caucus didn't come to life without controversy. We were called troublemakers and repeatedly challenged as to why we were in such a rush. It's true that we were challenging the status quo. And we were undeterred. We kept talking and meeting and looking for openings.

Southerners, for the most part, were solidly Democratic, chiefly because Abraham Lincoln was a Republican and the occupying army of Reconstructionists were Republicans. Reconstruction was that period from 1865 to 1867 when Federal troops and officials were garrisoned in the South to ensure the fullest implementation of the ending of the Civil War. Parenthetically, most African Americans were Republicans or voted Republican. The South was referred to as "the Solid South" for that reason. Although Harry Byrd Sr. had passed, his son occupied his seat as an independent, though he caucused with the Democrats so as not to lose seniority or party influence. Such was the situation in 1980 when the Democratic state convention was to meet in Roanoke. We chose that setting to make the presence of the Democratic Black Caucus known.

I called a friend in Roanoke who had some influence with the host committee to arrange a time and place for our caucus to meet. He warned me that the schedule was very tight, but he would give it a try—and he called me later to say that a room had been reserved for us at 5:00 p.m. on Friday of the convention. It was the only time available. I had no choice but to agree, although this was not a good time. Our members would be traveling by car or bus from across the state, and many working people could not be there until Saturday.

I had some concern that a poor showing would provide fodder for negative press, so I requested a small room, imagining how bad it would look if we had only a smattering of attendees in a large room. Instead, we were given the largest meeting room at the Hotel Roanoke.

To my amazement and gratification, when 5:00 came that Friday, the room was packed with over five hundred in attendance. That was the introduction of the Democratic Black Caucus to the rest of the Democratic Party and the beginning of the end for the era of the Byrd machine.

Sadly, today, most members of the legislature, and particularly the African American members, are really clueless as to what made the new Democratic Party of Virginia. The Democratic Black Caucus of Virginia, distinct from the Legislative Black Caucus, exists in name only.

By 1976, I was itching to stretch myself and to show that an African American could win a statewide election. I started putting out feelers about running for lieutenant governor in 1977. To my dismay, the *Richmond Afro-American*, which essentially served as the voice of our community, wrote that no African American should consider running for statewide office, stating that "most political observers believe that the chance of a black candidate winning in a statewide race is terribly slight in Virginia where conservatism runs high among whites and where the black vote is comparatively small."

I could not let this shameful defeatism stand. I sent a scathing letter to the editor. "I would like to believe that it was an unintentional negativism and would remind you that 'most political observers' have always been prophets of gloom and despair," I wrote. "They never thought blacks should run for any office, hold any office or aspire for other than that which was easily within their grasp. Virginia is no more or less conservative than we allow it to be. I would never consign black persons to the fate of what 'most political observers' think, whomever they may be."

I didn't run for statewide office that year, but the experience convinced me that our own spineless compliance with Byrd-era conventional wisdom was perhaps more damning to our cause than any prospective white racism. When I gave speeches, I often found myself straying from politics to encourage young African Americans to stand up for themselves and control their own destinies. There was a belief, often passed down from parents and grandparents, that young African Americans had to be twice as good and twice as qualified as their white counterparts in order to make it. I told them, "If you have to be twice as qualified, stop complaining and *be* twice as qualified. Do what needs to be done. Stop making excuses. The fault is not in our stars but in ourselves." It was tough talk, but it needed to be said.

One achievement of the Democratic Black Caucus was that it helped gather support for a young up-and-comer named Charles Robb. Robb, who was married to President Lyndon Johnson's daughter, Lynda Byrd, was considered to be a "new" Democrat—that is, not one beholden to the Byrd machine or to the old racial customs of the southern Democrats. African American support helped Robb win his race for lieutenant governor in 1977, and he knew he had me and the Democratic Black Caucus to thank. Four years later, we once again stepped up to help when Robb ran for governor.

Early in his campaign, I went to see him, carrying a checklist of items the Democratic Black Caucus wanted to see accomplished in his administration should he become governor. There were four straightforward but highly important points on the checklist:

1. Support for the creation of a state holiday honoring the birthday of Martin Luther King Jr.

2. Support for postcard registration, which would allow people to register to vote through the mail

3. A concerted effort to appoint women and minorities to positions in his administration

4. A promise not to support the use of public money or give tax relief to "charter schools" that were founded after the *Brown* decision to further delay and effectually block integration

We had our work cut out for us. Robb's opponent, J. Marshall Coleman, then attorney general, had gotten considerable support from the African American community because as a state senator, he'd supported my bill on the Martin Luther King Jr. holiday. On the other hand, the African American community knew little of Robb other than that he was the son-in-law of Lyndon Johnson, one of their heroes. Robb had never distinguished himself as lieutenant governor by being a voice for our community.

I took it upon myself to investigate Robb's record and positions in some detail and penned a lengthy letter on the Democratic Black Caucus of Virginia's letterhead, providing a point-by-point case for Robb based on his promising positions on everything from affirmative action to minority contractor initiatives to youth employment to voting rights. I highlighted his principled stand against limiting Medicaid funding for abortions for the poor. In this way, I gave Robb my wholehearted support and the support of my caucus. I felt that Coleman's crowing about his African American support was all smoke and mirrors. If he were elected, I expected more of the same—or worse.

To no one's surprise, the governor's race that year had an underlying racial tone. Just a week before the election, President Reagan made an appearance for Coleman in Richmond. One of the speakers on the platform that day was former governor Mills Godwin Jr., who, along with Harry Byrd Sr., had been at the forefront of the massive resistance strategy against the desegregation of public schools. In exchange for his backing, Godwin demanded that Coleman reverse his support for the Martin Luther King holiday legislation, and he did. At his appearance, Godwin criticized Robb's too-cozy relationship with African Americans, evidenced by his support for the items on my checklist. This performance shifted the tide of the African American vote. I worked with Robb's campaign to send out a letter signed by several dozen African American leaders from around the state supporting Robb's candidacy.

The question was this: Would our community show up to vote for Robb? I will never forget watching the returns come in on election night. We were all gathered at the legendary John Marshall Hotel, and early in the evening, Robb seemed to be doing well. Then panic coursed through the hall as the returns showed Robb losing by 100,000 votes.

A party chief from Norfolk sought me out and loudly blamed me. She shouted, "You and that damned letter! We would have been all right but for that!" I did not believe it for a minute. In fact, unlike others in the hall, I wasn't too worried about Robb's fate because I saw that the returns had not yet come in from heavily African American localities, especially the Northern Virginia precincts.

Before long, the results began to turn in Robb's favor. By the end of the night, he had won by 100,000 votes—aided by a heavy African American turnout. I believed then—and do now—that the letter had exactly the effect that was intended.

According to statisticians, Robb won 96.4 percent of the African American vote, and that's what put him over the top. Coleman's share was 3.6 percent, the third lowest on record. The lowest was Harry Byrd Jr. in 1970, with 3 percent, and the second lowest was Ronald Reagan in 1980, with 3.4 percent. As the total African American vote was nearly twice that of Robb's statewide victory margin, the numbers underscored its role in Robb's victory.

To his credit, Robb performed most of the checklist. I was convinced he was genuine. He never broke his word to me at any time during his governorship.

With Robb's election, the Byrd machine was crushed. Within months, Harry Byrd Jr. announced that he would not seek reelection to the U.S. Senate in 1982. And that's when things got interesting.

CHAPTER FOUR

Political Muscle

In the winter of 1982, Democratic Party leaders met to mull over candidates to replace Harry Byrd. I was at some of those meetings, and one name that seemed to be pushed to the front was Owen Pickett, a relatively unknown legislator who had served Virginia Beach in the House of Delegates since 1972 and had served as chairman of the Democratic Party. He was a quiet man, and I got along with him.

I was cautious about lending my support and the support of the Democratic Black Caucus. I wanted to know more about Pickett. But the party leaders were eager to get the show on the road. Pickett was their man. I wasn't in on the final decision to advance him as the Democratic candidate, although I didn't see any red flags either. But that soon changed.

On March 18, Pickett stepped up to the podium and announced that he was going to run for the U.S. Senate to replace Harry Byrd—and promptly stuck his foot in his mouth. Not only did he have kind words for the departing Harry Byrd Jr., but he spoke admiringly of Harry Byrd Sr., praising the lifelong opponent of the cause of equality for his independence and his stellar contribution on behalf of the state. That "independence" referred to his venomous fight against the *Brown* decision.

My heart sank. My conscience was aroused. In my view, Pickett's endorsement of Byrd tainted his candidacy with a century of Jim Crow. I could not let it stand. This was my obligation; it was also personal. I reflected back to how difficult it was for my father to speak about his parents' experience as slaves. But the one thing he didn't have trouble speaking about was the Byrd machine. For me, Byrd represented a backward drive to keep the Old South a bastion of white dominance. It baffled me that Pickett, who had never been particularly outspoken, would choose that opportunity to suggest that he intended to stand in Byrd's shadow. It seemed clear to me that Pickett was preparing to run as a conservative in the manner of Byrd.

Not wanting to fly off the handle, I paid Pickett the courtesy of a visit, and we had a long and cordial conversation. I tried to convey to him what Harry Byrd Sr. represented for African Americans and indeed for Virginia. Pickett was a nice enough guy, but he let me know he didn't plan on apologizing for his comments. He didn't think he needed to. His praise for Byrd, he explained, was not because of his racist ideology but because of his fiscal responsibility, which I thought was an interesting dodge but didn't pass the smell test. I wondered whether the history books would remember Byrd for his economic policies or for his massive resistance to integration.

Meanwhile, my phone was ringing with a reaction to Pickett's statement. Those calls came not just from African Americans but from whites too. Labor organizers called. The Virginia Education Association called. Before my eyes, I saw the storm rising, and I was in the thick of it. My supporters were telling me that if Pickett was to be the Democratic candidate, we had to run someone in opposition to him—and that person, they suggested, was me.

I called the governor. "This can't go on," I told him. "We can't support a man who says he's going to be like Byrd. This is serious."

"I'll talk to him," Robb said, and later that day, he called me back. "He said he's not going to change his statement or take back his comment about Byrd." To his credit, Robb was very unhappy about this, but I don't think he fully grasped how bad the situation was. Next, we appealed to

Robb to put pressure on Pickett to step down. Robb demurred, not wanting to upset the delicate balance of the new and the old Democratic Party. He appeared to be prepared to risk losing the African American vote, however, because I was going to run and take it with me.

I knew there was no chance I could win the party nomination against Pickett. But I considered running as an Independent. The first task was to get enough signatures on a petition to get my name on the ballot. Once that was done, I had an important decision to make. I told Robb, "It's very simple. If Pickett runs, I run. If he does not run, I don't run."

My goal was to demonstrate to Democrats in the most dramatic fashion that the old electoral coalition in Virginia was dead and buried, and if they believed they could win in 1982 without African Americans, Latinos, women, and progressives, they were free to give it a try.

On March 25, Robb invited me to the governor's office, where we sat down for a tense meeting. "If you run, we could lose," he said bluntly. I knew that, but I was holding firm. To reporters sniffing around, Robb said tersely, "Clearly, if Doug decides to become an active candidate in the general election in the fall, he would have a real impact on the outcome of the election."

I discouraged talk that Robb and I were enemies, but Robb had a big problem. As the titular head of the Democratic Party in Virginia, his job was to keep everyone in line. But I was straying and threatening to take a big chunk of the vote with me. Without the African American vote, the Democrat might lose, but I didn't think it was inevitable. "People should be careful about counting votes before they're cast," I warned.

I understood the stakes perfectly well. If my candidacy as an Independent swung the election to the Republican side, we could end up with a senator much worse than Pickett. It could also permanently destroy my status in the party and potentially put an end to my political career. At the very least I would be stripped of my seniority in the statehouse. I was standing pretty far out on a limb.

Among party insiders, there was little good to say about me those days. Noting that Robb had been a great supporter of African Americans and my threat to run was a slap in his face, my senate colleague from Fairfax, Adelard Brault, declared, "It just goes to show, you give somebody an inch and they want two miles. Wilder has been given a mile, and now he wants ten miles." This was a common criticism of African Americans that resonates to this day. We were always asking for "too much," as if we should be content with less and go along to get along as our advances trickled out on some majestic time line.

The old Byrd faction in the legislature was dismayed by my uppity behavior. Speaker A. L. Philpott just couldn't understand it, noting that "I've never had any trouble with these boys"—referring to African American members.

The governor sent Representative Alson Smith, the fast-food magnate and one of his key supporters, to have a talk with me. I was in a feisty mood, and I suggested we have lunch at his club—the whites-only Commonwealth Club. Embarrassed, Smith said, "You know we can't get reservations for the dining room." Of course I knew! I asked that we try the basement grill. I was friendly with some of the waiters there. Smith sighed. "Life's too short for me to be embarrassed by taking you to the Commonwealth Club," he said. "They don't like blacks up there." But my heart was flooded with anger and dismay because this was the truth of the matter, as clear as could be. The whole mess—the nomination of Pickett and the inability of an African American to dine in the center of Richmond—all came together. I said, "Okay, let's go to my club." I had recently been invited to become a member of the Jefferson-Lakeside Country Club as its first African American. It was traditionally a Jewish club. (They didn't like Jews too much at the hallowed old clubs either.)

Later, when the story hit the press, Smith was angry at me, and many people grumbled that I'd set him up by suggesting the Commonwealth Club. Perhaps. I wasn't beyond playing hardball.

It didn't matter what names they called me—and there were many: traitor, grandstander, coward, and narcissist along with, I'm sure, a few expletives. But I felt I had no choice. What seemed like a minor slip of the tongue on Pickett's part was a line in the sand for African American clout in Virginia. People had to understand that praising Byrd's independence meant approving massive resistance against the law of the land that protected us from segregation. We could no longer abide the mask of southern civility, the wink and a nod that protected foul beliefs. Time and again, the African Americans in the state had been called on, as if by Pied Pipers, to get out the vote for Democratic candidates—most recently Governor Robb himself. Yet after elections, they had a way of being forgotten.

My announcement that I was running as an Independent received national attention because there were no African Americans in the U.S. Senate at that time. As I had throughout my career, I made it clear that I wasn't running as a race-based candidate; I was running as the best candidate. I was tired of hearing the false praise from so many quarters that Pickett couldn't hold a candle to me—the unspoken conclusion being that if I were not African American, I would easily be the party's first choice.

As the nominating convention grew near, I held closed-door meetings with both the governor and Pickett. My recommendation was that both of us agree not to run—which had been my point all along. It finally worked. On May 4, Pickett withdrew his name. Robb made a statement: "It is with a profound sense of personal sadness that I concur in his judgment that the action is necessary to bring our party and our commonwealth back together." He also issued a statement praising me not only as the best and brightest but also as a loyal Democrat. He added, I thought gratuitously, "On the day that many expected him to launch an Independent bid for the United States Senate, Doug has instead sought to help reunite the Democratic Party. Like Owen Pickett yesterday, Doug has displayed the kind of political courage that has been instrumental in moving Virginia forward."

But both Robb and I knew that my political courage was displayed not in leaving the race—that was pragmatism and fairness—but in joining it in the first place. Relieved as he was that I withdrew my name, I'm not sure Robb ever looked at me the same way again. I had demonstrated a political muscle he hadn't fully appreciated, and he was somewhat wary about what I might do in the future. However, for the time being, the incident ironically cemented Robb's reputation as a party builder and enhanced his national stature. Robb later told a writer in reference to the Pickett affair, "I will probably always have a black mark against me for not somehow making that right." And yet he said, "I always thought that the strongest political act that I performed was to get both Pickett and Wilder out of the race."

As for me, I considered the Pickett withdrawal the first real display of what consolidation and sacrifice for the greater good could produce. Many thought that my political career was over. I was a pariah to some party loyalists, particularly in Pickett's Virginia Beach home area. During this era, the party was running scared after the tumultuous 1970s, when the liberal wing of the party drove many members into the Republican fold. Unity at all costs was the slogan of the day, but unity wasn't always the best policy when taking the long view.

The Democrats nominated Lieutenant Governor Richard Davis, and his campaign manager was none other than a fledgling political operative named James Carville. Three-term congressman Paul Trible was the Republican nominee. Trible was elected with 51 percent of the vote. He would serve one term. As he retired from the U.S. Senate, Harry Byrd Jr. told the Associated Press that he was leaving public service with his convictions and integrity intact. There wasn't a soul who didn't understand exactly what he meant by that.

For a long time after the election, many in the party blamed me for losing the election by causing a fuss, although I never believed it. Every candidate is responsible for making his or her case to the public, and Davis had not done that. In the end, I had won an important victory: Never again could the party afford to casually dismiss the African American vote.

As *Roanoke Times and World-News* reporter Dwayne Yancey wrote in his book *When Hell Froze Over: The Untold Story of Doug Wilder*, "Wilder was not simply black—he was brazen, and not afraid to shout 'racism' whenever it suited him. This was where Wilder's showdown with Pickett became so valuable. All the 'experts' had figured Wilder hurt himself by not being a team player in 1982. Instead, Wilder was now untouchable. Nobody wanted to make him mad." Yancey's version, while a bit exaggerated, had some truth to it. By daring to take a stand, I established myself as a person who wouldn't just go along to get along.

My political career has been a series of events like these. Often, I would have to risk everything—or, as they say in friendly poker games, "be willing to sleep in the streets"—to do what was right for the people. Time and again, pundits would step forth and announce that Virginia wasn't ready or that, to quote the great Virginia political scientist Larry Sabato in 1984, "I almost think the Democrats would be stronger electorally if they appeared to be standing up to some of those constituents."

I didn't agree. Those constituents, of course, are taxpayers and voters, ordinary people with real-life concerns and bedrock pride. It is those people who always stood with me for change in Virginia.

I will say that the Pickett affair made me known throughout the state. Before, I'd been a state senator from Richmond who happened to be African American. Now I was a politician with the stature to go toe-to-toe with the governor. People were a little more cautious about saying no to me, and in many cases, they were looking for ways to work with me. My decision to run for lieutenant governor in 1985 began to take form during those conversations.

In the new term after the election, I again rose to introduce a bill proposing a King holiday. By that point, King already had a holiday in seventeen states. The march of progress was making the appeal an inevitability, whether my colleagues thought so or not. At least now we had a governor in Robb who would sign the bill if it passed the legislature.

Once again, the bill was defeated. I vowed to bring it to the floor again the following year. In April 1984, it finally came to pass. Robb called me and suggested we do the bill signing at Virginia Union University. And so, on the 119th anniversary of General Robert E. Lee's surrender of Confederate forces at Appomattox, Governor Robb signed the bill calling for a King holiday in Virginia. It was an incredibly emotional day and a high point of my legislative career.

Martin Luther King Day had become a federal holiday the previous year, but in Virginia, we did it a little differently. All holidays in Virginia, with the obvious exception of those like Christmas, Thanksgiving, and the Fourth of July, were celebrated on Mondays, so in an insane turn of events that would have had all parties turning over in their graves, the holiday, celebrated on a Monday, was called Lee-Jackson-King Day, and it would be celebrated that way until 2000, when the holidays were divided. It perfectly symbolized the psychic divide that characterized the South. After 2000, Lee-Jackson Day was celebrated on the Friday before the Monday celebrating Martin Luther King Day. It was a long weekend.

The success of the King holiday showed the change that was occurring in the Old Dominion. At last, Virginia was ready—and so was I.

CHAPTER FIVE

Re-Digging the Well

THERE IS A STORY IN THE BIBLE THAT TELLS OF ISAAC, THE SON OF Abraham, faced with a terrible drought in the land. He complained to God that all the wells had run dry and that there was no water to feed the crops. And God instructed him, "You must re-dig the wells that your father dug."

As I looked at my life and my public obligation, I thought often of that biblical story. The leaders of the civil rights movement, great people like Martin Luther King Jr., had dug the wells, releasing the springs of equality. But the water supply wasn't eternal. Wells run dry. And it was up to us to re-dig them. That understanding of personal responsibility had propelled me into politics, and now, at the age of fifty-four, I had decided to dig a deeper well—to become the first African American elected to statewide office in Virginia.

It wasn't easily done. When in mid-1984 I announced my intention to run for lieutenant governor in the 1985 election, almost nobody thought I could pull it off. Once again, the consensus was that I was unelectable—and it wasn't because I lacked stature, experience, or ability. Members of my own party were afraid I'd drag down the entire ticket or, worse, cause a split government. In Virginia, the slate of state candidates was a threesome—governor, lieutenant governor, and attorney general—but we each had to carry our own election. It is therefore possible that the governor and lieutenant governor can be from different parties.

Fearing a loss, Democratic Party power brokers began cautiously reaching out to me. With flattering words, kindly demeanors, and an abundance of lip service to my achievements, they tried every which way to talk me out of running. There were some sweetheart offers if I would consider abandoning my candidacy. One involved making me party chairman and giving me access to a private plane.

In December, University of Virginia political scientist Larry Sabato said my chances of winning were one in a hundred, and more likely I'd sink the ticket. And in the process, he said, I'd accuse anyone who didn't vote for me of being racist. It wasn't a just accusation. That wasn't my style. (And, in fairness to Sabato, he later admitted that he'd been wrong.)

It's a truth in politics that sometimes it's more difficult to corral your friends than to defeat your enemies. Early meetings of my supporters were chaotic and inflammatory. The mood in those rooms was fearful, as speaker after speaker demanded that I prove I was up to the task of running statewide. With amazement, I realized that my own supporters didn't fully believe in my chances, and they were hedging their bets in ways I found wearying. Sometimes I snapped back when my own "friends" made vague disparagements. Considering my perfect record of winning senate elections, the hand-wringing seemed out of place. But there it was.

I was furious when Robb's press secretary was quoted in the *Washington Post* saying about a Wilder candidacy, "For better or worse, this is still Virginia. That makes it very difficult." Well, what the hell did he mean by *that*? I called Robb and asked him why his press secretary was disparaging my chances. Robb tried to brush it off by assuring me that his press secretary was speaking for himself, not for Robb. I shot back that a governor's press secretary *never* speaks for himself.

While the party desperately tried to find someone to run against me, several people were vying for the top spot. Robb remained hugely popular, but in Virginia, the governor could serve for only one term. The front-runners to replace Robb were Lieutenant Governor Richard Davis (who had lost to Trible in the 1992 U.S. Senate election) and Attorney General Gerald Baliles, a centrist who reminded many people of Robb. Davis and Baliles waged a heated campaign. I favored Baliles, and I was able to do some things that helped him. I met privately with him, and we concocted a strategy wherein he emerged as a winner despite Davis being endorsed by labor, most African Americans, and liberals.

Unopposed was the third member of the ticket, the candidate for attorney general. In another first for Virginia, that was Mary Sue Terry, a former member of the Virginia House and an assistant commonwealth attorney for Patrick County. A popular woman with rural roots, Terry once joked that her hometown was so small that the high school taught driver's ed and sex ed in the same car—a rare funny line from a woman who wasn't known for her humor.

The Republicans were also slugging it out. For the longest time, the front-runner for governor was Marshall Coleman, who had lost to Robb in 1981. Some people were a little bit nervous about a do-over, even after Coleman commissioned a poll showing he could easily beat any of the Democratic front-runners. His chief opponent was Wyatt Durrette, a hard-liner in the mold of Ronald Reagan. The front-runner for lieutenant governor was state senator John Chichester from Fredericksburg. Durrette and Chichester would ultimately prevail and be nominated. I heard people say that if Chichester had a pulse on election day, he'd beat me.

In one unsettling turn of events, Owen Pickett's name started to appear in the press as a possible Democratic contender for lieutenant governor. Pickett said that if my campaign collapsed, he'd accept a draft. I tried not to pay much attention, but I knew what was going on. In a troubling interview, Pickett said, "Unfortunately, I sense racism creeping into voting patterns, and if my perception is correct, putting a black man on the ticket would crystallize that feeling." An editorial in the *Virginian-Pilot* got it right that the draft talk was meant "to keep the Anyone But Doug Wilder movement alive."

Robb always assured me he was pulling strings for me behind the scenes but explained that, as governor, he had to stay publicly neutral. I didn't buy it. He had a way of damning me with faint praise and of down-playing me in the interests of being fair to others. Criticizing those who might want to make the campaign about race (or, in Mary Sue Terry's case, gender), Robb publicly demanded that they challenge us on *merit*. In a press conference, he as good as invited others to come into the race and show their stuff. Later, he assured me he did it for my benefit. If that was a favor . . .

Meanwhile, the media was regularly leaking anonymously voiced concerns from party leaders who feared that my candidacy might bring down the entire ticket. Their cowardice made me furious. I alone among all candidates had to defend my reason for running in spite of my fifteen-year record of service. I had an inkling about why. The Mondale–Ferraro presidential ticket had just been trounced by Rea-gan–Bush, and the Monday morning quarterbacks critiquing our party suggested that we had become too much of a "rainbow," too interested in quotas above quality. I understood that for some people, an African American on a ticket was automatically a quota candidate. I was not discouraged by this terrible falsehood. The only way to change hearts and minds was to run and show them differently—and to address the cowardice head-on.

A *Daily Press* editorial compared the hand-wringing of my party to the "salesman who assures his white customers, mock-confidentially, that an all-white crew will install their new air conditioning. The salesman may be a racist, or he may not. What is certain is that he knows that he will close more sales than he will lose by assuming his customers make choices based on racist judgments. . . . Unfortunately, when it comes to race prejudices, the political brokers have shown the same opinion of the electorate as that air-conditioning salesman has of his customers; they figure to win more often than lose by assuming the worst."

With lackluster support from Robb and members of the state Demo-cratic Leadership Conference regularly urging me to leave the race "for the good of the party," I needed a game changer. I found one in the per-sonage of a thirty-five-year-old shaggy-haired New York Jew named Paul

Goldman. Goldman was an unusual choice to consult on a statewide campaign in Virginia. A Yankee liberal, offbeat, and rudely combative, he slammed up against southern gentility. But I liked him. He might have been crazy, but he was crazy like a fox. He was a brilliant political strategist, and I responded to his fearlessness. If I was going to do this, I was willing to go all the way. Goldman and I made an odd couple, but he appealed to the fighter in me.

Goldman was a hardball player, and so was I. We decided that the racial issue, lingering beneath the surface, had to be brought to light and neutralized. So when the presumptive Republican candidate for governor, Wyatt Durrette, called me a liberal not in the tradition of Virginia and called my candidacy "controversial," I spoke up and said "liberal" was a code word for "race." A lot of party people, including Robb, didn't like me saying that. They thought I was picking an unnecessary fight and playing into the other side's hands. The fear of the "angry black man" ran deep. But it was actually a calculated move, one that effectively helped take the liberal charge off the table. During my first debate with Chichester, I selected fifty-four prominent bills where Durrette's vote was identical to mine. I asked which of these bills was "liberal." Chichester could not answer the question. From then on, people were very careful about labeling me a liberal for fear of being called racist.

After all the anxiety that preceded it, the Democratic nominating convention was uneventful. The Baliles–Wilder–Terry ticket was easily approved. I knew I had to give the speech of my life to bring the doubters on board. I also wanted to tell a story of who I was—to summon up the experience of my fifty-four years and in the process arouse the passions of the crowd:

Just a mile from this very site, I was a young boy growing up and playing on the cobblestone streets of Church Hill. Back then, who would have thought that someday he would rise to head the Senate Transportation Committee and be responsible for all the roads, highways, and mass transit facilities in the commonwealth of Virginia?

Back in the 1950s, when I served my country, I was unable to participate in the affairs of my state government. When I wanted to become a lawyer, I was forced to go to school outside of the state because the laws didn't permit me to attend a Virginia law school.

Who would have thought that in the lifetime of that young soldier, he would rise to become chairman of the Senate Privileges and Elections Committee, responsible for writing all the election laws in Virginia?

When I entered the senate in 1970, I was rated forty out of forty. Who would have believed that in the career of that freshman legislator, he would rise in the judgment of his peers, both Republicans and Democrats, to become ranked as one of the five most effective lawmakers of the 140-member General Assembly?

And who would have thought that all that has occasioned in these past years would occur in my lifetime, to where today in this great coliseum, in a hall filled with the party that has controlled the General Assembly during this century, that I would be standing here as the Democratic nominee for the office of lieutenant governor of the commonwealth of Virginia?

The cheers of the crowd told me I had achieved my goal. For the first time, I felt the party was with me. There was no turning back. Now I had to go out and win it.

While others were waging their campaigns by plane across Virginia, Paul Goldman had a different idea for me—a two-month, four-thousand-mile trip by land through every county, town, and back road of the state. My nephew Michael was enlisted to drive the station wagon that would serve as my campaign "bus," and my son Larry, a law student, accompanied me. I still have the wall-size map detailing every stop of the tour through the heart of Virginia.

We decided to start in the southwest—the rural coal belt in the shadow of the Appalachian Mountains. Although heavily Democratic, no one could predict—least of all me—how I would be received by the good ol' boys there. I figured I was a good ol' boy too, every bit a son of Virginia, and that's the way I would play it.

Although southwestern Virginia was the antithesis of urban Richmond and the north, I had one edge. They weren't used to having politicians come courting, and this sign of respect didn't go unnoticed. My trip, especially given my race, was newsworthy enough that a press contingent followed me, and I enjoyed plenty of free publicity.

The early weeks of my tour were among the most inspiring of my political career. In markets, gas stations, parking lots, farms, banks, factories, restaurants, gun shops, beauty parlors, street corners, schools, mines, and pool halls, everyone was friendly and wanted to meet me. I extended my hand again and again, and it was taken every time, firmly and warmly. No one mentioned race. We were just folks talking about our lives. When prodded by reporters to say whether they could vote for an African American, most people just shrugged and replied that they'd never before had an opportunity to do so.

I was under no illusions; the press followed me because they were expecting—and even hoping for—a brawl. A face-off with the Confederacy would have made a good story. But it never happened, and they were forced to report a different story entirely.

My message was not "I'm an African American trying to win your vote." It was "I'm a Virginian trying to win your vote." If there's such a thing as color blindness—and I don't believe there is—it could seem that way playing pool with the ol' boys or chatting about their needs with locals in the tiny towns that dotted the state.

To those who said it was too soon to elect an African American lieutenant governor, I found that the state was ready. The people were ready. During my tour, I almost never stayed in a hotel. I stayed in people's homes—even whites—and they were thrilled to host me. Word passed that I was in town, that I was staying with so and so, and they'd come out. We never had an escort; we just arrived in small towns and got to work. The people felt the connection so deeply that years and even decades later when I traveled to that part of the state, people would come up to me and greet me with a touching familiarity. They'd show me pictures I took with them that they considered cherished possessions. They'd tell me, "I was twenty years old when you came out, and I sent you $50."

Without the tour, I'd never have been elected. People want to know who you are, and many Virginia politicians as good as ignored parts of the state. I always went out there and shook every hand, and I didn't presume to know what people thought until they told me themselves. I remember once at a country store, I was walking around shaking hands and came to a man sitting on a barrel. As I shook his hand, he said, "I thought you were going to pass me by."

"No, sir," I said with a smile.

"I got something I got to say," he continued. Half expecting a diatribe, I was taken aback when he launched into a heated defense of a woman's right to choose abortion. "Ain't no man's business anyway, is it?" he concluded.

I grinned. "You're absolutely right."

I was moved by the simple faith these rural people had in government. I saw how little they had and how much they needed. They just wanted someone to listen and to care—to pitch in and re-dig that well.

Late in the tour, my journey took me to the home turf of speaker A. L. Philpott, who had been my nemesis for many years. Philpott was the "Old South"—not shy about occasionally using the "N" word. He'd been one of my fiercest opponents on the Martin Luther King birthday, and he'd once referred to blacks in the legislature as "boys." But I wanted his endorsement.

We were nervous about reaching out to him, but finally Paul called and said, "We're coming your way and would like to meet with you in your office."

Philpott nearly knocked Paul back in his chair when he replied, "Not enough. We're going to host a breakfast, and I'm going to pay for it." The press showed up in force, and Philpott got up in front of everyone and stood next to me while the photographers clicked away. "This will be a great experiment for Virginia," he told the crowd—a bit cringe-worthy, but I didn't mind. His endorsement and the photograph were worth it all.

When it was my turn to speak, I laid it on the line: "To the pundits, to the naysayers, to those who said it could never happen, we are here together today," I said. "To those who said it never could be, we are gathered here today to march on to victory." I told the audience about my experience going into places where the Confederate flag hung high and how at those places I was warmly greeted and even embraced. I joked that if that was what I'd find under a Confederate flag, I'd like to know where I could find more of them. The crowd laughed appreciatively. We were all on the same page at that moment.

I felt exhilarated by the tour. I was where I wanted to be—close to the people. But not everyone was so enamored. A story in the *Times-Dispatch* put it bluntly: "Wilder is hurting himself with corn-pone campaign stops at virtually every dot on the map," it stated, suggesting that I should have been concentrating on raising money instead. Maybe so, but I have to say that going out among the people felt right to me. If a politician won't do that, what good is he?

Chichester's campaign had been relatively quiet while I was on tour, but finally in September he came out swinging. The first lob was to say I was soft on crime, which was a familiar Republican canard but happened to be a poor issue against me because I actually had a record that told otherwise. Chichester's rhetoric was over the top. He said I had the criminals' interests at heart.

He then published an ad that asked, "Why Did Doug Wilder Neglect the Needs of Battered Women?" He was referring to my opposition to a 1982 bill giving magistrates the power to evict abusive husbands. I thought the bill was poorly drawn—an opinion shared, incidentally, by most Republicans. In any case, the ad never got much play because two of Virginia's largest newspapers refused to run it on the grounds that it was misleading.

The problem was that the Republicans lacked a strong line of attack against any of us. They also seemed not to have a positive platform of their own. In Chichester's case, I saw that he never gave voters a reason for his candidacy other than that he wasn't me. In some races, that can be enough—but not this one. From the outset, he made the calculation that anyone with a beating heart could defeat me, and he barely registered on the scene in the early months, springing to life only later to go overboard with his attacks. In the final months, the mud began to be slung.

An editorial in the *Virginian-Pilot* called Chichester desperate: "By constantly distorting Senator Wilder's record, the Chichester campaign has steadily lost credibility. More and more Republicans lament the underhanded attacks against Senator Wilder. Mr. Chichester has done little to advance his standing in the minds of thoughtful voters."

The tragedy for Chichester was that he was known as a decent guy who hated negative campaigning. Events swept him along in a direction he didn't want to go. With the mudslinging growing constant, I had to decide how to respond. Paul wanted me to be a fighter and go negative. Although I never ducked a fight, my instinct was to stay above the fray.

But some statements couldn't go unchallenged. In a September speech, former governor Mills Godwin stepped in it with a denigrating line he never intended to get much play: "I have a hard time seeing how Jerry Baliles could espouse the record of this man [referring to me]. Why, he actually introduced a bill to repeal the state song." Suddenly, race was back in the picture. The Republicans were horrified. No one wanted to go there. By that point, the song incident was long forgotten, and people preferred mostly to keep it that way. They didn't want to be reminded of the Old Dominion. I told the *Roanoke Times and World-News*, "In keeping with the positive tone of my campaign, I think it is best left in the past. I don't intend to go back fifteen, one hundred, three hundred years to talk about what used to happen in Virginia. I'm concerned with moving on." Durrette plummeted nine points in the polls in the days following Godwin's remark.

The rightward swing of the state Republicans was a problem for a party that had traditionally been the moderate response to Byrd's machine. During the campaign, I heard rumors that former governor

Linwood Holton, who continued to be a leader in the moderate wing of the Republican Party, privately favored me in the election. According to *Virginia in the Vanguard: Political Leadership in the 400-Year-Old Cradle of American Democracy, 1981–2006*, Holton, who had been silent about whether he would endorse Durrette for governor, said that he would do so only if Durrette repudiated Godwin and the Byrd organization. That never happened.

In spite of the success of the tour and the generally positive press, most pundits were still opining that I didn't have a chance of winning. They acknowledged that I had impressive legislative experience, that I understood the issues, and that people liked me. It's just that I couldn't win. But I had a finale planned, an ace in the hole: the cop.

I had run a shoestring campaign with the plan of spending most of my capital on television in the final weeks. And the centerpiece of that ad campaign was a thirty-second spot featuring a small-town white cop named Joe Alder.

It had been Paul's idea to put together a law-and-order ad, and when we were on our tour through Lunenburg County in the south-central part of the state, we gathered up some local deputies and tried to film a commercial. It was not going well. It just didn't feel authentic. Then Joe Alder walked out of the nearby courthouse, wearing his uniform, and stopped to watch us. Alder was the very picture of a small-town southern cop—white, burly, tough, with a honeyed drawl. But beneath his stereo-typical appearance, he was a thoughtful, politically astute guy. And he was planning to vote for me. We convinced Alder to do the spot, and at the end of the campaign, it was Alder's face and message resonating across the state: "I'm a working policeman. I put my life on the line every day. That's why we need people in public office we can trust. . . . The Fraternal Order of Police endorses Doug Wilder for lieutenant governor."

That ad played all over Virginia, effectively diffusing the law-and-order charge, except among the true believers.

Race continued to be downplayed in the election until Durrette and Chichester got a very big endorsement from none other than Harry Byrd

Jr. in a letter to the *Times-Dispatch*. Byrd implied that my candidacy was instrumental in his decision. No surprise there! He said he was worried about my being "a heartbeat away" from the governor's office. To be honest, I didn't mind Byrd's endorsement going to my opponent. He was preaching to the converted of his own "church," and they weren't going to vote for me anyway. Likewise, it certainly didn't help them when Senator Strom Thurmond of South Carolina stumped for the Durrette–Chichester ticket across Virginia.

The Republicans were calling in all the big guns. On October 9, President Reagan motorcaded across the bridge to Arlington, where he was the headliner at an event for Durrette. Reporters noticed that the mood at the event wasn't upbeat. The polls weren't looking good for the Republican ticket. Reagan had flowery words for Durrette's ethics, faith, family values, and so on, but in many ways, the speech didn't fit the mood or circumstances. Reagan joked, "You know, back in 1977, I spoke at my first fund-raiser for Wyatt, and by coincidence the day of the fund-raiser just happened to be my birthday. So, the event turned into a kind of a dual celebration. There I was thirty-nine years old—for the twenty-seventh time. Wyatt, I just want to make sure that when I reach forty next year, you can give me a birthday call from the governor's office." Everyone laughed thinly. Reagan's appearance was always a charm offensive, and it surely helped encourage Durrette supporters, but it probably didn't earn him many new ones. Ranks were closing fast in the final month.

With only two weeks to go to the election, the Chichester campaign amped up the negativity, producing ads that gut punched me on character issues. Once again, Paul was ready for a fight. He begged me to hit back. But I wasn't so sure. The decision whether to go negative was one of the toughest of my campaign. It's painful to be attacked—no question about that. But I had always believed that my greatest strength was my positivity. Robb and others agreed that negative ads could backfire badly. Paul persisted. Finally, after searching my soul and speaking to many of my friends and advisers, I decided that, win or lose, I was going to be myself and stay on the high road. My decision made for a tense finale, as my lead slipped and the numbers tightened.

‑‑‑

Many Virginia residents remember November 4, 1985, for its history-making election. Others remember it for the Election Day Floods, a devastating storm that landed in the state in the wake of Hurricane Juan to the south. In the days before the election, torrential rains swelled rivers in the western part of the state, destroying crops, closing roads, destroying thousands of homes and businesses, and killing more than twenty people. Among the hardest-hit areas was Roanoke, where the Roanoke River rose to over eighteen feet and flooded the community. Many residents were stranded and had to be airlifted from cars and properties by helicopters.

By election day, the rain had abated, and hastily organized makeshift polling sites were set up. But voting was down in the western part of the state—the hand of God reaching down and upsetting the best-laid plans of Republicans and Democrats.

The polls were predicting a Democratic sweep in the state, but I wasn't ready to do a victory lap until the votes were counted. Throughout the day, I kept hearing about a lower turnout than the last gubernatorial election, and the most disturbing thing was that African Americans weren't turning out in the high numbers we expected either. God knows, we needed their vote to be strong.

Every politician will understand what I mean when I say that election day is a day of raw nerves. All that can be done has been done. The organization of the ground game is in place. The most important task of a candidate is to go to the polls and vote and then walk around and talk to the people, shaking hands and expressing thanks. On election day, my daughter Loren said to me, "Dad, I want you to win this to show them they're wrong about you and Virginia." I smiled at her. I hoped that not *that* many people were wrong about me. I had reason to feel some optimism, but I didn't let myself even harbor a thought about victory. Victory would come, if it did. Later, I noticed that a reporter had written I was ebullient on election day. More likely, I was relieved that the long drive was over and filled with gratitude for the number of people who believed in me.

The election night party was to be held at a locale I knew quite well—the John Marshall Hotel. It was there I had waited tables as a young man and listened to the white businessmen make jokes at my expense. It was there I was invisible to the powerful establishment—just a boy serving them. They felt no embarrassment about telling racial jokes in my presence.

As I sat with Baliles, Terry, and Robb in a suite upstairs at the John Marshall awaiting the final election results, I could feel the thrumming roar of hundreds of people jammed into the ballroom below. I was nervous. Despite the polls, I never felt victory was in my pocket. I was confident that Baliles and Terry would win, but my race was much tighter. My thoughts traveled back to the state tour, to the warm handshakes and cordial greetings, to all the promises, and I hoped to God I could count on their being real. And to be honest, I had my private fears as well. I had grown up in Byrd's Virginia, where the machine had the ability to make things happen on election day. In my imagination, I could picture thousands of Wilder votes floating down the swollen Roanoke River.

You have to have an iron gut to survive election night returns, and this was particularly true in my case. Throughout the evening, the numbers went up and down in a dizzying cascade of uncertainty. Long after Baliles and Terry's victories were assured, my race went uncalled. By 10:30, it looked like I was winning, but the AP and UPI were silent. There were signs, though—were there ever! One was a huge victory in Buchanan County on the farthest western tip of the state. It was one of the whitest counties in the South, and according to Daniel J. Sharfstein's essay "The Secret History of Race in the United States" for the *Yale Law Journal*, between 1880 and 1930, more lynchings occurred there than in any other part of the state. Yet in 1985, Buchanan County gave me twice as many votes as Chichester.

When the results piled up in our favor and Baliles and Terry were declared winners, there was plenty of cheering and backslapping in the suite. Although the numbers showed me in the lead, I was still hanging back, waiting for the call. "Let's go," Robb cried, motioning us to the door. "They're waiting for us downstairs."

"Just a little while longer," I said, pulling back. "We want to be sure."

"Come on, Doug, the election has been won." Robb was impatient, and so were Baliles and Terry. The hour was late, and the mob downstairs was restless. I kept dawdling, taking trips to the bathroom, and straightening my tie, as Robb simmered and the roar continued below. Finally, at just past 10:30, we got into an elevator and headed down. When we reached the bottom, we learned that the AP had just called a Democratic sweep.

We elbowed our way into the hall, where the crowd was roaring and leaping. I'd never before seen so many souls pressed together in one place—not to mention so many jubilant African American faces at the John Marshall. We piled onto the stage—the winning trio of Baliles, Terry, and me, along with Robb, as Robb happily took the microphone to introduce us, fighting to be heard above the din.

When it was my turn to speak, my remarks were extemporaneous. I spoke from the heart. "I could not begin to tell you how happy, how pleased, how thrilled I am with this moment. Many, many years ago in this room . . . when I used to listen to political speeches as I would wait tables on this floor as well as in the gallery, little did I believe one day I just might be your lieutenant governor." I ended with the truest line of all: "I am proud to be a Virginian."

〜

When the votes were tallied, they showed Baliles with 55.2 percent of the vote, Terry with 61.4 percent of the vote, and me with 51.8 percent of the vote. We captured the youth vote, the African American vote, and a large percentage of the women's vote. While it was no surprise that I lost the white vote to Chichester, I received a healthy 44 percent for an African American, and almost 75 percent of the people voting for me were white. As Sabato observed, "Wilder campaigned not as a Jesse Jackson, concentrating his time and attention on the black community, but rather as a Tom Bradley (the Los Angeles mayor)—a mainstream black candidate widely acceptable to whites. The success of Wilder's strategy is clearly reflected in the 44 percent of the white vote he secured." It was a decisive win that I hope predicted the advent of the New Dominion.

It's hard to overstate what the victory meant to the people of the state, especially African Americans. Gayle Perkins Atkins, editorial director of WRC-TV, captured the sentiment beautifully in a moving editorial:

Someone who was with me from my birth was dealt a mortal blow last week. He is an ominous fellow who had a lot of power at one time, enough power to keep me—and others like me—from deciding at various stages of my life where I could be born, live, eat, go to the bathroom, go to school, work and be buried. He controlled not only these tangible things in my life, but also the intangibles that caused the most pain. And he did this not only in Virginia, but in much of the South. This person has been in a weakened state for a while, although some have tried to revive him. But he was absent last Tuesday. His name is Jim Crow.

Lots of people were backtracking on their predictions of doom. Sabato, who had said I had a one-in-a-hundred chance of winning, now told a reporter, "I am willing to eat my share of the crow, but I would appreciate some company. I don't like dining alone."

After the election, the party leaders didn't hesitate to take credit for my victory. The Democratic Leadership Council (DLC) was particularly outspoken about its role. Time and again, it was said that Robb's benevolent hand had reached out from the governor's office to guide me to success, laying the groundwork for making an African American acceptable in Virginia. This was not exactly the way I saw it. Some people's memories may have softened in the glow of the victory, but mine had not. I hadn't forgotten how hard I had to fight the "Anything But Doug Wilder" elements in my party and how hard they had worked to convince

I was precocious at an early age. PRIVATE COLLECTION - L.D. WILDER

On the porch of the family house in Richmond which my father had built.

My brother Bob was my hero. He always let me come along on his exploits.

At fifteen I was ready to take on the world—or at least the folks at the barbershop.

I was drafted into the army in 1952 during the Korean War.

Sergeant Wilder, outside my hootchie in Korea.

At the State Capitol in 1969. Dr. William Ferguson Reid, Richmond-Henrico, (middle), was elected two years before me to the House of Delegates, becoming the first African-American elected to that body since reconstruction. Dr. William P. Robinson, Sr., Norfolk, was elected to the House of Delegates the same year as I. 1969.

My family—my wife Eunice and our three children, Larry, Loren, and Lynn. The marriage didn't last, but we were always proud of our remarkable kids.
PRIVATE COLLECTION - L.D. WILDER

A moment of reflection with our family German Shepherd, Kaiser, by my side. PRIVATE COLLECTION - L.D. WILDER

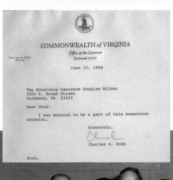

I was an upstart in my early days in the Virginia Senate, but eventually became an important player and power broker.
PRIVATE COLLECTION - L.D. WILDER

I fought for a Martin Luther King, Jr. state holiday throughout my senate career. Finally, in 1984, Governor Chuck Robb signed the bill into law.
REGGIE JENKINS, PHOTOGRAPHER FOR GOVERNOR ROBB, THE LIBRARY OF VIRGINIA

My predecessor, Governor Gerald Baliles and I didn't always see eye to eye, but he supported me when I ran for governor.

On January 14, 1990, surrounded by my children, I was inaugurated as the first African American Governor of Virginia. It was my proudest day.

I was a single man in the Governor's Mansion, which meant late nights at my desk.
RICH PIERMARINI, PHOTOGRAPHER FOR GOVERNOR WILDER, THE LIBRARY OF VIRGINIA

As Governor, I gave a weekly radio address.

Nelson Mandela and I had a warm meeting in New York City before the Democratic National Convention in 1992. His courage and positive spirit remained an inspiration to me.

Newly elected President Bill Clinton paid me a visit at the Governor's Mansion.
RICH PIERMARINI, PHOTOGRAPHER FOR GOVERNOR WILDER, THE LIBRARY OF VIRGINIA

When Mikhail Gorbachev visited Virginia in 1993, he praised our Founding
Father, Thomas Jefferson.

As our first African American president, Barack Obama is an inspiration, but I've never hesitated to share my views and even challenge him on issues I care about.
PHOTO COURTESY OF B. J. WILEY

As governor, I had an opportunity to host many important world figures in Virginia. It was a special honor when Prince Charles visited the Governor's Mansion.

RICH PIERMARINI, PHOTOGRAPHER FOR GOVERNOR WILDER, THE LIBRARY OF VIRGINIA

I've always believed in education as a pathway to success. Here I am as Governor at my *alma mater*, Virginia Union University.

other candidates to run against me. I hadn't forgotten how Robb constantly criticized me during the campaign, chafing at my refusal to run the kind of big-ticket operation he favored. Paul and I did not want a campaign bureaucracy but a shoestring, close-to-the-ground operation, and it worked. I hadn't won because the Democratic Party had stirred up a magic brew or waved an anointing wand. I won because I went out and appealed to the people. Had it been up to the DLC, I never would have been nominated. This was especially galling to Paul, who didn't hesitate to go to the press to complain that Robb was getting too much credit for my win.

God knew I had no control over Paul, but he wasn't wrong, and I said so. Many among the DLC leadership felt that the party was hurt by its association with minorities and women. Getting me elected was definitely not solely or even mostly their doing.

Robb reacted to my remarks in a very startling and personal way. One day, I received a long letter from him—six pages, single spaced—full of hurt feelings and recriminations. He detailed his many contributions to my success and complained that I had not properly credited him. It showed a thin-skinned side to Robb. "Friends don't treat friends like you've treated me recently," he wrote. He then went on to detail what he felt were my flaws as a candidate, particularly my lack of organizational skills. "We were very lucky reporters never focused on [my organization] as a measure of basic management ability in assessing your potential for governor if the need ever arose." It was not the kind of letter one expects to receive in the aftermath of a historic victory.

I didn't respond. I figured it takes two to argue, and I wasn't interested. I was also, quite frankly, discomfited by the underlying threat in the letter. Robb implied that if I didn't change my tone, he and others just might walk away from me the next time around. He wrote, "I am very much concerned with the way you have treated me, and have more reason to be concerned than others. We've always regarded you as a friend and ally. . . . Whatever the cause of your present feelings, I think it is important that we have a serious talk like the ones we had so often and so amicably up until a few days after you were elected lieutenant governor. We would like to try to resolve our differences. Please let me know your intentions."

My silence was my answer.

It didn't help relations that I wasn't sitting quietly in my office as lieutenant governor. A lot of people expect the lieutenant governor to be a potted plant, showing up to preside over the state senate and echo the governor's talking points. Anyone who knows me will realize that I wasn't going to settle for a nonrole. I could be more centrist—some said conservative—than the governor and my party, especially on taxes and crime. My stance on those issues received so much play that Larry Sabato joked, "Just as I predicted, John Chichester won." That was far from the truth, but my years in the senate had given me a good grounding in fiscal common sense.

As a result, I had a couple of public differences with Governor Baliles. Early on, I challenged him on raising sales taxes to pay for an ambitious transportation program. I looked at the bill and saw that it was going to raise just about every tax you could name and said, "Hey, wait a minute. I didn't sign on for that." I had served as chairman of the Transportation Committee for years. I think I knew as much about transportation issues in Virginia as anybody. As lieutenant governor, I had to rule on the germaneness of an issue that came before the assembly, and I ruled that the governor's request was not germane. The tax package Baliles was proposing to pay for the road project seemed regressive to me, too burdensome to the middle and lower classes. I made my strong feelings known. Although Baliles and I mostly had a very cordial relationship, he was unhappy on this occasion, believing I'd pulled the rug out from under his big initiative.

After I opposed the sales tax hike, Robb sent me a second angry letter, accusing me of not being a team player. He wrote, "Your credibility with most key participants in the political process is disappearing rapidly, and many who have supported you in the past are no longer sure you can be trusted."

Again, I didn't respond. I was astonished when Robb then released both letters to the press. I thought it made him look bad. Of course, the press ate it up. Here was a personal controversy that reporters could sink their teeth into with relish. I was disgusted. Why on earth would Robb start a public fight with me? It wasn't as if he were planning to leave politics. He'd need my support again, just as he had in the past, but I would not be bullied into it. In the wake of damaging press coverage, I finally reached out, and Robb and I sat down for a meeting at his home in McLean. We at least made the appearance of a truce, but the whole matter bothers me to this day. And, unfortunately, it wouldn't be the end of our conflicts.

Many people treat politics like a game, where you wrestle to get on top. I wasn't concerned with besting Robb and never had been. Nor was I overly concerned with being known as a "team player." In sixteen years in the senate, I had collaborated and compromised many times, and I fully understood that was the way to get things done. But I always maintained my independence when it came to principles. Robb never liked that about me, and he often warned me about the damage I could cause when I strayed from the party line.

I had a reputation for liking a fight, but I always thought they got me wrong. I was never a firebrand. The real story is that I was independent. I saw things my way, and I followed my own path. Being a team player is overrated when it means diluting things down to wishy-washy mush.

But it seemed as if Robb's letters were sending me a message: "If there is any alternative to you, that's who the party is going to back for governor in 1989."

CHAPTER SIX

Virginia Is Ready

THE "ANYONE BUT DOUG WILDER" CAMPAIGN WAS IN FULL GEAR IN 1988 as I began to prepare my run for the governor's office. I don't say that bitterly or angrily. It was just a fact—right out in the open for everyone, including the media, to dissect and discuss. However, I was ready to run, and, more important, I believed the state was ready for me. Being lieutenant governor was crucial to that calculation. The people of Virginia had needed to see me in action, to develop a comfort with me. They needed evidence that I reflected their values and ideals, and I believe I gave it to them.

By every accepted measure, including being the lieutenant governor, I was the natural heir to the nomination. I had proven my ability to win on a statewide level. I had a constituency. But as I'd learned in 1985, my party still had reservations about me. Was it my race? My independence? Probably some of each. I'm not suggesting that the party leaders were themselves racist. We'd crossed that bridge. However, they were nervous about the electorate and didn't fully trust that the broad constituency that had elected me lieutenant governor in 1985 would take the extra step to make me their governor.

There remained what I call a chloroform of doubt—a cloud that threatened to stagnate progress with the question "Is Virginia ready?" It was almost as if they needed a pronouncement from on high that the time was right for voters to elect an African American governor. Anything short of a divine proclamation would not do. But I had learned growing up that if the cause was right, the time was always right. You couldn't wait around until everyone got comfortable.

Perhaps there was concern that the African American electorate in Virginia was only 15 percent, not enough to drive my election. But if I had been depending on my own race, I never would have run for lieutenant governor, and I wouldn't run for governor. I was depending on having a message that appealed to the majority of the electorate.

As for my independence, Robb's words of warning about losing the trust of the party leaders still resonated with me. They didn't like the way I'd run my 1985 campaign—never mind that I won. My failure to abide by the master rulebook gave them agita. They never fully understood me. I wasn't driven by a desperate need to be elected or even by the desire to be accepted. Being one of the boys, a member of the club, never enticed me, as I had spent half my life on the outside and learned to make my own way and keep my own conscience. Those old habits did not desert me once I entered politics. Any victory would have been hollow if I had won it by leaving myself behind.

In 1988, the Democratic Party in Virginia was pretty much controlled by the will of two men: Chuck Robb, who was running what would be a successful campaign for the U.S. Senate and who was quite popular (people were calling it the "Robb era"), and Governor Baliles. My tiff with Robb was still a lingering bruise, and in spite of our cordiality, I had no illusions about our relationship. Baliles and I had our differences as well. While neither Robb nor Baliles ever said publicly that they didn't want me to be the party's candidate, there was a lot of effort behind the scenes to find an alternative.

The pot was being stirred.

Early in 1988, the word started leaking out in the media that Attorney General Mary Sue Terry was considering a run for governor. Many top money donors and lobbyists publicly declared their support for

Terry. Two key operatives—Al Smith, the chairman of the Democratic Legislative Caucus, and Allen Diamonstein, the state Democratic chairman—publicly declared their support for Terry. I knew they believed that her electability was high since she'd won in 1985 by such a wide margin. However, her record in office was not seamless. She was just getting comfortable in her job when she began to be heralded as the great white hope (in the vernacular of the day).

At forty, Terry had proved herself to be a loyal Democrat with a strong constituent base, and she might have made an attractive candidate. She raised and spent a considerable amount of money. I never had a question whether I would be able to secure the nomination. But you can tell things about politicians in terms of their ambitions. Terry didn't seem to know how to approach being governor in spite of the groundswell of advisers urging her to run. Her potential candidacy made headlines for a month or so before it ended. In March 1988, Terry held a press conference to make an emotional announcement that she would not be running for governor but would seek reelection as attorney general. She called me beforehand to tell me the news personally, and with that, the path to my nomination seemed secure.

Governor Baliles was a pragmatic politician. I think he realized that if the party was seen to be divided over its nominee, especially when I was so obviously an electable candidate, we might lose the race altogether. He quietly began to make it clear that he thought I was the obvious candidate—the one who could win. In fact, he couldn't have made it clearer. At a commencement speech at Norfolk State University, an African American school, he walked up to the podium and began to speak about me:

Three years ago, Doug Wilder ran for lieutenant governor of Virginia. Many told him he could not win. He politely ignored them. He drew his resources and took his case to the voters. He relentlessly debated the issues. He talked not of the past, but of the future. And he won. Now, Doug Wilder has his sights set on a new office, a higher office, an office with which I have some familiarity. Again, some will tell him he cannot win. Again, he will politely ignore them. Again, Doug Wilder will draw together his resources and take his case to the voters. Again, he will address the future. And again, he will have a chance to make history in Virginia.

Baliles insisted it wasn't a formal endorsement, but that didn't matter. It was as good as one. Those circling around my candidacy suddenly stopped. The simple, realistic calculation was hardening: They knew I could win. Suddenly people were looking at me with new eyes.

But before I could think too hard about launching my campaign, there was another election to win. In Virginia, the governor's race happens on an off year. But the "on" year of 1988 was very much in play, with our party's candidate, Chuck Robb, running for the U.S. Senate. Paul Trible had stunned the Republican Party with the announcement that he would not seek reelection in 1988, an almost unprecedented defection, and Robb, who was immensely popular in the state, was running for the seat. Robb probably would have run even if Trible had stayed in, but now the election seemed like a walk in the park for him. The Republicans never found a viable candidate—I think in large part because no one wanted to take on Robb. They nominated Maurice Dawkins, a sixty-seven-year-old African American minister, who was virtually unknown in the state, and Robb won the Senate seat with 71 percent of the vote. It was a remarkable achievement in a year when Democrats didn't fare too well in the South and the country elected another Republican president, George H. W. Bush.

Jesse Jackson's strong showing in the 1988 Democratic primaries helped me as voter registration efforts added new voters to the rolls. However, when Jackson won the Virginia primary with 45 percent of the vote, many mainstream Virginians were inclined to associate our party with far-left liberalism. I had to get my centrist message out against a tidal wave of anti-Jackson sentiment.

Throughout 1988, any potential competition for my nomination fell away, and it looked as if I would be unopposed. I was receiving signals from top fund-raisers that I could have whatever I needed. The reason was twofold. First, no one doubted my ability, not just to win but also to govern. Second, there was a sense of history that the time was right, that people wanted to back progress. No African American had ever been elected governor anywhere in the nation, and many people were captivated with the idea of such a first. That was not, however, my focus. It was the same as in 1985, when I made a point of saying I wasn't running a "black" campaign.

Some of my constituency didn't like that. They wanted me to be a Jesse Jackson–style candidate. But in my view, African American issues weren't really *black* issues. They were people issues—issues involving people who were disproportionately affected because of race but not confined to them. I would make the same speech to a Chamber of Congress meeting or a group of coal miners that I would to a Baptist church or an NAACP gathering. I resisted the pressure to be divisive, and I was never divided in my own mind. I was buoyed by surveys conducted inside and outside my campaign that showed three impressive facts:

- 61 percent of whites thought of me as a man of honesty and integrity.

- 60 percent of whites believed I was qualified to be governor.

- 60 percent of whites regarded me as an independent leader.

On the Republican side, there was a crowded field in the early days. At the front was the perennial candidate, Marshall Coleman, who was still boasting about his past ability to get a decent (for a Republican) share of the African American vote. Paul Trible, who had initially said he was leaving the Senate to spend more time with his family, entered the race, showing that a run for governor had been his intention all along. Trible was to the right of Coleman, but he wasn't as popular, and many believed he'd not made much of a mark in the Senate—unless you counted his criticism of Oliver North when he appeared before the Senate panel investigating selling arms to Iran, which didn't endear him to fellow Republicans.

Many within the Republican Party felt that Trible had scammed them by not running for reelection to the Senate since they promptly lost the seat to Robb. Also exploring a run was Congressman Stan Parris, from Northern Virginia, who was not well known throughout the state. With so many candidates, there was a debate that year about whether to abide by the tradition of nominating the candidate at a convention or to hold an open primary. Republicans opted to hold a primary, only the second time in history that the party did so—the last time being 1949.

This was good and bad news for the party. As every candidate who has ever run in a contested election knows, a drawn-out primary campaign can leave scars on the eventual victor. On the other hand, by taking their case to the people in a primary, Republicans had a chance to shape the narrative for the election campaign.

Still, it was nice to be out of the ring for once. As the Republican candidates hammered each other, the Democrats were showing a rare spirit of togetherness. I was eager to mend the fences with the DLC, knowing that my remarks in 1985 had not been forgotten. "I may have been wrong in some of my assessments," I acknowledged carefully. This was like repairing hurt feelings in a family spat.

For most of the Republican primary season, Trible held the lead. But as the primary neared, Coleman was barreling back with biting attack ads flooding Virginia's airwaves. Parris, who continued to run third, also spent most of his capital attacking Trible. One of Coleman's most effective charges against Trible related to an event from Trible's 1982 Senate campaign when he made a classic misstep. Barely covered at the time, Coleman pulled it out of the archive and went to town. During that campaign, to show his support for the military, Trible had appeared next to a fighter jet wearing an Air Force pilot's flight suit, although Trible had never served in the military, having received a medical deferment during Vietnam. Coleman exploited the incident, calling it a lack of integrity that Trible would appear wearing a uniform he'd never earned the right to wear. I think it hurt Trible with conservative Virginia voters, whose regard for military service was reverential. It made Trible look like a phony and probably tilted the vote to Coleman.

By June 7, the *Washington Post* was calling the race a dead heat between Trible and Coleman. Days before the Republican primary, my party held its convention at the Richmond civic center to nominate its ticket, which, in its diversity, was a repeat of the makeup in 1985: an African American at the head (me), a woman for attorney general (Mary Sue Terry running for reelection), and a white man, Donald Beyer, a political newcomer, for lieutenant governor. My presumptive nomination drew press from across the country. It was estimated that some one hundred reporters were on hand to see history being made.

I felt moved and immensely satisfied when first Baliles and then Robb rose to nominate me. Baliles evoked roars of laughter and cheers when he said of me, "When I think of Doug, I think of a poem written more than a hundred years ago. It says, 'Voyager upon life's sea, to yourself be true. And whate'er your lot may be, paddle your own canoe.' Well, I've looked out the window of the governor's office on more than one occasion and, sure enough, there was Doug paddling by. But he was nice about it. He always waved."

Robb got up and spoke frankly about the fact that we'd had disagreements. He even mentioned those damn letters. But, he said, "Our differences and those letters represent only one year in a relationship that has spanned fourteen years. . . . Don't let anybody make any mistake about this race. I'm back in Doug's corner in 1989."

When it was my turn, I looked out over the convention crowd of over four thousand people and spoke from the heart: "I have seen Virginia learn and grow, and in my lifetime, I have learned and I have grown. I have learned that big dreams are born of big dreams and that big dreams become realities only when the brow is willing to sweat and only when the principled commitment runs deep." Larry Sabato, reflecting on my nomination, noted, "It was a measure of how far Virginia politics, or at least the Democratic Party had come in four years."

And so my campaign was launched with a simple slogan: "We've come too far to turn back now." The message wasn't just about electing an African American governor. It was about the emerging face of Virginia as a new progressive state. The collapse of the Byrd organization ushered in a new era, and that was undeniable, but there were other signs of change. Virginia was now considered an opportunity state with a growing economy. Unemployment was at 3 percent. The Corporation for Enterprise Development ranked us among the fastest-growing and most diverse state economies, with an "A" in economic performance. Virginia was also helped by its proximity to the nation's capital, with a constantly fresh infusion of jobs, population, and enterprise. It needed wise leadership to steer it through the coming years.

As had happened so many times in the past, Robb managed to give me a kick under the auspices of praising me. Or maybe he just wasn't thinking straight when he mentioned at a luncheon that Coleman would be the toughest man for me to beat. I often wondered if his comments swayed some undecided voters to back Coleman. On November 12, Coleman won the nomination. Maybe Republicans thought—thanks to Robb—that he'd have a better chance of beating me. (I actually thought Trible was the tougher opponent.)

Everyone was predicting a ruthlessly negative campaign, and many people advised me to come out swinging. The example of Mike Dukakis was lingering in the air after 1988. Many people believed he'd lost the presidential election because he didn't give a forceful response to the famous Willie Horton ad. Willie Horton was in prison serving a life sentence for murder when he was let out of jail for a weekend furlough program that Governor Dukakis had instituted. He didn't return after the weekend and ultimately committed other crimes, including rape. The Bush campaign tied Horton to Dukakis in a powerful race-baiting ad. As Lee Atwater, who was Bush's campaign manager, put it, "By the time we're finished, they're going to wonder whether Willie Horton is Dukakis's running mate." The Dukakis campaign never fought back, and he was stuck with the image. Pundits speculated that if Dukakis had played dirtier, he might not have lost. Maybe, maybe not. But I thought it was cynical and unworthy of a candidate to think that the only way to win was to play dirty.

I decided to wage a positive campaign, but I made it clear that I would not hesitate to fight back when I was attacked. I was not afraid of campaign mud or outright assaults based on my race. I remembered well how Durrette had lost nine points against Baliles after former governor Godwin's ill-considered remarks at a campaign luncheon.

It was hardly surprising that Coleman's first attack, days after his nomination, was that I was soft on crime—a common Republican method of wrapping up race, liberalism, and spinelessness into a neat package. It was so predictable, it was almost as if they were on automatic pilot. The problem was that it was completely unwarranted. I'd taken plenty of criticism from the liberal wing of my own party about my support of the death penalty for those who murdered police officers. On principle, I was not opposed to the death penalty, just to what I considered an inequitable application. Early in my career, I had opposed the death penalty based solely on the fact that it was not imposed fairly. From 1901 to 1962, 236 people were executed in Virginia. Only thirty-four were not African American and impoverished. But the laws had been strengthened to be fairer, and I was now comfortable not opposing the death penalty. In fact, I often took law-and-order positions. But the Republican playbook was written with such favorite charges.

I expected to do battle on issues such as the economy and crime, but right out of the gate, abortion unexpectedly became a central issue of the campaign when the Supreme Court ruled in *Webster v. Reproductive Health Services*, giving states leeway on abortion restrictions. Suddenly, abortion was being passionately debated on the state level. Coleman, who had once declared himself pro-choice, was now as far to the right on the issue as one could get. During the primary, he had spoken about his belief that life begins at the moment of conception, that abortion should be banned, and that no allowances should be made for rape and incest. This radical change of stance on abortion was a trend that was sweeping the Republican Party. President Bush himself had been a supporter of choice on abortion for most of his political life but had "evolved" by the time he ran for president in 1988 as antiabortion. Opposition to abortion remains a Republican issue to this day.

I made it clear that I would not be wavering from my long-standing support for a woman's right to choose. My position was that decisions about abortion should be left to women in consultation with their doctors, families, and religious advisers. When a reporter asked me what I would tell one of my own daughters if she were to get pregnant and ask my advice, I replied that I'd tell her, "It's your decision."

Not only was my position morally supportable, but it also reflected the view of the majority. Our own polling showed that an overwhelming majority of Virginians were opposed to placing restrictions on abortion beyond parental notification. A further *New York Times*/CBS poll showed that only 17 percent of voters were in favor of banning abortion. Coleman's harsh antiabortion stand, perhaps instrumental in winning the primary, placed him in a perilous position of being against something most people wanted. I hammered him on abortion throughout the campaign because he was vulnerable. It wasn't just that he was veering far to the right of public sentiment. Coleman never seemed to have his heart in the fight to ban abortion. Voters are good at spotting inauthenticity, and I'm sure they picked up on it.

⁓

I was eager to get on the road again, repeating my four-thousand-mile tour that had been such a remarkable experience when I ran for lieutenant governor. I planned to once again visit every byway, town, and village across the state. This time, my "bus" was a minivan. My son Larry would once again accompany me, and once again we would stay in private homes.

Perhaps realizing how effective grassroots campaigning was for me, Coleman's campaign cried foul on my statewide trip, complaining that I was purposely absenting myself from media scrutiny—in effect *fleeing* into the far corners of the state. It was a very odd charge. Did Coleman not believe that people in rural communities deserved as much face time as those in the media markets? Did he not see the heavy press contingent that followed me? And why wasn't *he* out in the state? His communications director acknowledged that campaigning in small towns was a "worthy" endeavor, but I should stay home. I saw it as more than just worthy. It was the essence of a campaign to meet the voters on their own turf.

From the start, the trip had a different character than my first one, for two reasons: I was now a sitting lieutenant governor, so I had to answer for the administration, and there was a major coal strike going on in western Virginia. I was the only candidate willing to walk into that volatile arena. Perhaps Coleman's reluctance to visit this part of the state was a fear of meeting angry miners.

Since April, the United Mine Workers had been striking against Pittston Coal Group, the Pennsylvania company that ran the largest mining operation in Virginia. It had been a nightmare for our administration, which had to balance support for the miners with the need to maintain law and order. Governor Baliles had sent hundreds of state troopers to keep the fragile peace. Thousands of strikers had been arrested, and the situation was fraught with tension and the threat of violence. My advisers were nervous about my walking into that powder keg, but I still felt a close connection with the people of those mining communities, who had welcomed me so warmly in 1985. I wanted to hear about the situation from them personally. And so, in the heat of summer, I drove through the towns of southwestern Virginia to meet the people on their own turf.

The sentiment I encountered was hard to hear. Miners felt betrayed by an administration they had supported so faithfully. I heard the same thing again and again: "We came out and backed Baliles 100 percent when he ran for governor, and where is he when we need him?" As they saw it, the only thing coming out of the governor's office during the strike crisis was overreach by state troopers. They thought law enforcement, at the behest of the governor, had been too heavy-handed, treating them like dogs. They told me they felt as if they lived in an occupied territory, and the fever of resentment was high. Some stores and restaurants refused to serve state troopers. When I arrived in their midst, they wanted to know from me which side I was on.

The miners told me that they were committed to nonviolence and complained that most of the arrests were made while they were congregating peacefully—as one of them pointedly added, "Just like Martin Luther King."

I had the difficult task of voicing support for the cause of the miners and for the unions while also being tough about law and order and trying to communicate the administration's thinking. The depth of personal agony was immeasurable. They were putting their families' futures on the line because they had no choice. It was either that or be powerless against the coal companies, who held most of the cards. Solving their problem was beyond my scope. I couldn't write the contract that would appease both sides. So I listened.

It was a delicate balancing act. I wasn't fully in support of the way Baliles was handling the crisis, but I had to speak carefully so as not to make our disagreement the story. At the same time, I had to show these people why they should trust me to be on their side if I were governor. I had only my history to stand on. When I talked to people, I reminded them that whenever the rights of poor working people had been on the line, I'd been there—and I would be again. My personal history put me in their corner. I spoke to them sincerely, with a full appreciation of their pain. "I know the emotions that grip you," I told them. "I know the strife that occurs when brother is against brother. That's not good, not good for any of us." The strike dragged on, but my outreach paid off. On election day, I carried all five of the coal counties.

One controversy emerged later in the campaign as a result of my trip. It was dubbed "Wilder-gate" by some members of the press. Coleman's campaign got hold of an alleged tape recording between me and members of the United Mine Workers that purportedly showed I was willing to take down the state's right-to-work law, which prevented compulsory union membership. This was a controversial issue. Virginia had a long history as a right-to-work state.

The edited transcript that was released was a setup that distorted my position. I had never wavered in my support for the right-to-work law. I was unable to learn the source of the tape, but Coleman's campaign liberally used the controversy a week before election day, seeking to upend my campaign. One newspaper editorially stated that it was crazy to suggest that I had met privately with union people who were on strike to make that promise. My sympathy with the United Mine Workers was strong. But I never considered challenging Virginia's right-to-work heritage. In fact, once I was governor, I maintained the same position.

As I was finishing my tour, an event occurred in Virginia Beach that stole the headlines for days. Greekfest was a traditional Labor Day celebration. It was originally a relatively tame festival, but over the years, it had grown so large that it now attracted as many as 50,000 students and young people, mostly African American, to the beachfront community. This year, with pressure from the local community, alarmed city leaders had decided to show a heavy police presence. The students reported that they felt constantly harassed, and the tensions building throughout the weekend finally erupted Sunday. The National Guard was sent in, and the clashes went on for two days. In the end, rioting destroyed over one hundred stores and restaurants and closed down the community.

I spent Labor Day at parades in Buena Vista and Covington near the Blue Ridge Mountains. When the smoke cleared, everyone was asking the same question: "What will this mean for Doug Wilder's campaign?"

Responding to the Greekfest riot was a tightrope walk because the sides had already aligned in a simple racial formula: The students claimed that the riot was in response to racism in the community and heavy-handed tactics by the police and National Guard. White residents claimed that the students were behaving like thugs and threatening their community. I had learned (and it's been demonstrated repeatedly since) that when there is a black–white clash, it's almost impossible to address it in a reasoned way.

I knew people would want a response, but I refused to be drawn into it. I reiterated something I had said many times—that violence was not to be tolerated. The NAACP and others wanted me to go after the police, but I felt that the last thing anyone—including me—needed to do was to make it the topic of a political campaign. I called for a full investigation of events and urged that we leave it up to investigators. That wasn't enough for some national commentators who seemed to think that because I was African American, I was personally responsible for addressing the matter. Pat Buchanan announced on television that the Virginia Beach violence was going to finish off my campaign.

Decades later, in 2014, when white students rioted in New Hampshire during Halloween partying, they were described as kids being kids, and there was very little public outcry. The double standard was obvious. When white students misbehaved, they were kids. When African American students misbehaved, they were thugs and rioters. Yet in both instances, I had the same view: Rioting, destruction of property, and violence are never warranted, whatever the race of the perpetrators. In a civilized society, we handle our disputes in the courts, in the press, and at the ballot box.

As we entered the fall, Paul Goldman reported some problems with our existing campaign manager, someone Paul himself had recommended. He sometimes spoke without authority, and it began to be troubling. At the same time, a young man from Northern Virginia appeared at my office ready to do everything he could for the campaign, including making a $15,000 donation—a considerable sum in those days. His name was Mark Warner. Warner was thirty-four, and he'd already made a fortune in the cellular phone business. He told me straight out that he was interested in possibly running for office someday, but first he wanted to learn the ropes and help me get elected.

Warner improved the campaign structure by showing we were willing to make a change. It looked good and made a difference. However, he also knew that his political inexperience would not license him to do things without consulting us. Four years earlier, we'd taken a lot of flak for running a seat-of-the-pants operation, but it worked for us. Now we needed a more structured approach, and Warner helped us step up our game. He was particularly skilled at building coalitions with business leaders. Let me add that although Warner has stated on any number of occasions that he managed my campaign and he did have the title, Paul, Frank Grier (who handled media), and I made the day-to-day campaign decisions. However, I could see that Warner had political talent. I believed his role in my campaign would help him with his future aspirations, and I think he'd agree that it did. He went on to make a career in Democratic politics—first as governor and then as U.S. senator.

Meanwhile, I was honing the key theme of my campaign—an appeal to "Virginia's New Mainstream." My opponents thought they could paint me in narrow ways, call me liberal, and say I had extreme views. But I wanted to make it perfectly clear that *they* were the extremists. I was confident that the people of Virginia longed for a clear path to the future—one that was progressive and economically sound.

⌐◦⌐

By October, we were circling back to the abortion issue, which became heated during a debate sponsored by the League of Women Voters. That day, new polls were reporting me well ahead of Coleman, which didn't help his mood. I believed Coleman was vulnerable on abortion. During a point in the debate where we were allowed to address questions directly to each other, I asked Coleman a hypothetical: If a bill came to his desk as governor restricting abortions in cases of rape or incest, would he sign it?

Coleman was angry, and he accused me of being disingenuous for even raising the question. "You know, there's not a single legislative supporter who would even introduce the bill. It is a false fear," he argued.

I pushed back. "What would you do if the bill came to your desk *miraculously*?"

Again, he didn't answer the question I asked but rather said, "I don't believe abortion should be used for birth control or sex selection of the child."

But we weren't talking about that. We were talking about rape and incest. And Coleman simply would not answer the question. I didn't buy the argument that it didn't matter how one stood on an issue because it would never come to your desk. How can anyone say that with a straight face? And Coleman's frequent claim that I supported abortion as a means of birth control or for the purpose of sex selection was a ludicrous invention.

I put out my position in two very strong ads. The first featured an American flag as the backdrop to my words: "In Virginia we have a strong tradition of freedom and individual liberty—rights that are now in danger in the race for governor. On the issue of abortion, Marshall Coleman wants to take away your right to choose and give it to the politicians. He wants to go back to outlawing abortion, even in cases of rape and incest. Doug Wilder believes the government shouldn't interfere in your right to choose. He wants to keep the politicians out of your personal life. Don't let Marshall Coleman take us back. To keep Virginia moving forward Doug Wilder is the clear choice."

The second ad showed how abortion could be a crossover issue, especially for pro-choice women. It used a fifty-seven-year-old female publishing executive who stated, "In the past, I have voted Republican, but this November I'm voting for Doug Wilder. Marshall Coleman wants to take away the right of a woman to choose, even for poor women who are the victim of rape and incest."

Race had not come up in the campaign from either side, but toward the end, with the polls tight and me showing a stubborn lead, Coleman began to let the racial implications seep into the campaign. He started complaining that I was being given a pass by the media because I was African American—that the media narrative was too full of presenting my election as historic. He was bitter about what he called a double standard. His point was completely transparent, and I had to laugh when I listened to it. If I was being treated with kid gloves by the media, it was news to me! No candidate had faced greater scrutiny than I had—not just during this campaign but for years.

But Coleman decided to go there. A week before the election, he stated publicly that he didn't care how much history my election would make. "I for one am not going to stand by and watch a person who is unfit glide into office with a feel good, make history message." Although he kept insisting that a double standard applied to my campaign, when pressed to explain exactly what he was referring to, he stopped short of saying it was because of race—although the point was obvious.

The "special treatment" claim rankled, being reminiscent of the typical complaint that African Americans were coddled by affirmative action. Coleman was saying, in effect, that my election would be the height of affirmative action—a dog whistle to the resentment felt by some segments of the white population.

Should I respond? Some of my advisers were urging me to go after him and bring race out in the open. I refused to do it. I was intent on making the final days uplifting. Overall, I had tried to fulfill my promise to avoid a negative campaign. Many of my ads presented a positive message and focused on my vision and character, while Coleman's ads were almost entirely devoted to attacking me.

As a sign of his desperation, he pulled out the old "row house" story, which had been popping up for years whenever my political opponents wanted to hit below the belt. In 1975, I had purchased an investment property in Church Hill with the thought that one of my children would eventually live in it. It remained empty and undeveloped, as my life became busy. Some of the neighbors, who were friends of Coleman's, complained, though, and a grand jury was impaneled to determine whether it was a "nuisance." The grand jury ruled that it was not. I finally sold the property in 1984 before I became lieutenant governor because my children were living away from the city. My opponents liked to paint the picture of me driving around in a Cadillac while this property I owned was in disrepair. They thought it was a useful campaign optic. In any case, I hadn't owned the property for years when Coleman brought it up in a debate. All I could do was throw up my hands and say, "I really can't believe you're still chewing on that old rag." It was annoying, but it also showed me that Coleman was digging around at the bottom of his campaign bag, anxious to find something—*anything*—he could use against me.

Through it all, race was still not an open issue, which was less surprising than it might have seemed. The *Wall Street Journal* analyzed the situation this way: "Race is seldom mentioned by either candidate. But the prospect of a black man in the governor's mansion in Richmond has, for more than most politicians and commentators admit, skewed the political calculus of a state long ruled by tobacco gentry, textile barons of a dozen rural crossroads, a tiny band of editorialists that chew on the philosophy of John C. Calhoun and Harry Byrd's political machine, which deliberately kept voter turnout small, white and easy to manipulate."

———

Days before the election, the *Washington Post* reported the stunning news that its poll showed me leading 52 to 37 percent. I'm not superstitious, but that poll sent a shiver down my back. Could it possibly be true? I didn't think so. The poll was an outlier, its margin much larger than the average, which was around nine points. I believed that the result would be closer still but that we would prevail. My advisers were optimistic, but some warned that it was going to be close. We just never imagined how close, even though our internal polls showed us to be always within plus or minus two percentage points, which was within the margin of error.

Every campaign reaches a point when the candidate steps back to let the voters speak, and the ground-game troops rush forward to make sure they do so. Our get-out-the-vote organization was the best in state history, with huge phone banks and armies of "doorbellers" canvasing the state. Turnout was exceptionally high on election day. Some exit polls were predicting a landslide.

That evening, my supporters were gathering in the Richmond Marriott Hotel. At my suite at the Commonwealth Park Hotel it was a nerve-wracking, up-and-down night. The first results from AP showed a large lead, but then they backtracked, saying there was a reporting error. Some precincts had been counted twice. Suddenly, my early lead nearly dissolved, even as Beyer and Terry were winning their seats by landslides. While my aides, family, and friends stared with agony at the flashing television reports, I kept calm and even upbeat. I felt I was going to win, but my life didn't depend on it. I had to repeat many times that evening, "Don't worry. Don't worry."

A week earlier, the *Washington Post* had me ahead by fifteen points, but in the course of election day, my lead had evaporated. What happened?

One explanation was a phenomenon later described as the "Wilder effect," previously known as the "Bradley effect." In 1982, Mayor Tom Bradley of Los Angeles had run for governor of California and was widely predicted to win comfortably. When a majority of white "undecided" voters broke for the white candidate, he lost the election. Analysis showed that many white voters who said they were voting for Bradley then voted for his white opponent. It was believed that they answered polling questions untruthfully, not wanting to seem biased against an African American candidate. This was in the back of our minds as we watched the numbers tighten to a dead heat on election night. It was further supported by the fact that Beyer and Terry were easily winning their races, with evidence of massive ticket splitting.

That being said, the margin of victory is not as important as the victory itself, and by 11:00 p.m., ahead by a few thousand votes, the race was called for me. I waited for a concession call from Coleman, but it didn't come. I had called Larry Sabato to see what precincts still needed to report and given his reports, I knew I had won. The race was never called for me, but finally, I rose to my feet. "It's time to head over to the Marriott," I said. Just before 11:30, I took the stage to the cheers of hundreds of supporters. People were emotional, tears streaming down their faces. They were drained from an evening of high drama and ecstatic with the final result.

"I am here to claim to be the next governor of Virginia," I announced in a ringing voice. "We've come this distance because people prior to our coming believed in what we could do." As they gazed up at me with such joy and trust that it made my heart swell, I told them how as a child when I read Thomas Jefferson's words that all men are created equal, I knew it meant me. And I felt a little choked up recounting it because I was thinking about my mother. *She* was the reason I knew it. Finally, I told them how proud I was to be a Virginian. And I was. Always had been but especially on that night.

When I finished, I turned to my aides who informed me that Coleman was at the Omni Hotel telling his supporters that the race was not over. The early gloom of the night had lifted in his hotel room when the AP reported its mistake and his totals climbed. Now he was holding out for another accident of fate. Although the race was called for me, Coleman never did concede that night or in the coming days. Coleman said he would not concede until the votes were canvassed, and he also said he might ask for a recount.

I chose to get started with my transition team and to respond to the many appeals for me to speak and sit for interviews. Some people might have been paralyzed by the uncertainty or challenged by the dampening effect of the lack of a formal assertion but not I. I felt a renewed energy and resolve.

The canvass result that affirmed my victory wasn't announced until November 20. The final tally had me winning by only 6,741 votes—less than four-tenths of 1 percent. There was an unprecedented amount of ticket splitting—voters who chose Coleman for governor but Beyer and/ or Terry for the other spots. Terry got 63 percent of the vote, and Beyer, who was an unknown, inexperienced politician, received 54 percent.

It would be disingenuous to suggest that race was not a factor. There's plenty of evidence that the Wilder effect explained the discrepancy between the polls and the vote, but one follow-up poll by the *Richmond Times-Dispatch* was especially striking. It showed that 56 percent said they *had* voted for me, a numerical impossibility demonstrating that the Wilder effect was operative even after the election. As the paper observed wryly, nothing succeeds like success. It's also relevant that the other prominent African American candidate to win that day, David Dinkins as mayor of New York City, experienced the same thing. Dinkins was comfortably ahead in the polls but won by a very narrow margin. That is not to say that the difference was racially motivated, only that there was a racial component in the answers given to pollsters, especially when the questions were asked face-to-face.

Perhaps the answer could be capsulized in an old joke that made the rounds during those years:

How many Virginians does it take to screw in a lightbulb?
Five. One to change the lightbulb and four to reminisce about
how great the old lightbulb was.

Progress is slow, and we'd come far. But the commitment to going forward wasn't universal. On November 20, when Marshall Coleman picked up the phone and called me with congratulations, I knew we were on our way. As Larry Sabato said so well, "Nineteen-eighty-nine was the real thing. For Virginia, even by a tiny margin, to become the first American state to elect a black governor was electric. Never has a state election drawn so many international news organizations. It was headline news around the world that a state so identified with the old Confederacy had broken this key barrier." Sabato also told the *New York Times* that the race issue had been suppressed during the campaign because Virginians didn't want to embarrass themselves. Perhaps that was true, although I felt the election was far more profound than that. In my mind, race was not a prominent issue because the people of Virginia had already moved past it, laying down the heavy burden imposed upon them by the likes of Harry Flood Byrd. They were eager to claim their place in the future, free of ugly biases that had stalled our state's progress. I was merely the conduit by which they voiced a consensus that was already there.

The 1989 election also delivered a message to Republicans about the growing fracture in the party. Coleman received a historically low percentage of votes from his own party, and according to Sabato's analysis, about a third of my votes came from people who had voted for President Bush in the 1988 election as well as a quarter of those who identified themselves as conservatives. For me, that also meant I would be serving under a big tent.

❦

January 14 was an extremely cold, windy day in Richmond, with the temperature near the freezing mark. That didn't stop nearly 30,000 people from making their way to Capitol Square to witness my inauguration. Coatless and hatless, I didn't feel the cold.

I looked out on the crowd—my people, the people of Virginia. African American faces were in abundance, tears streaking their cheeks. News reports said that more African Americans than whites were in the crowd, and that is understandable. Like me, many of them had grown up in a setting where their color stood between them and the ability to move freely in society. My sisters were present, as were my children. I would have given the world to see my mother's face, and my father's, and my brother Bob's, along with those of my other departed siblings. They deserved this moment as much as I ever could. It was hard not to remember the way things used to be, and the thought was bittersweet because of all those who had not lived to see this day.

Across Capitol Square stood a bronze statue honoring Harry Flood Byrd Sr. and another honoring General Stonewall Jackson. The Old Dominion still looked down at us from those pedestals, but we were the living, breathing emblems of the New Dominion.

Standing beside me was Supreme Court Justice Lewis Powell, a native of Richmond, who would administer the oath of office. We had been friends for years, and for me Powell represented everything that was good and strong about our state. I wanted him beside me at this significant moment for our state. In ill health, there was a chance Powell wouldn't be able to make it, but heavily bundled against the cold, he was there, and he told me he wouldn't have missed it for the world. I was grateful.

As I placed my hand on the family Bible to take my oath, I felt confident that my inauguration was signaling more than the much-heralded "first." I had won not because of my race but because, being African American, I had succeeded in making my case to the people. To the roar of thousands of voices, I stepped up to speak to the people of Virginia, hoping that I could present a vision that would inspire them for the coming four years:

Four years ago, I stood on this spot to assume the second-highest office in the commonwealth. Today, because of your faith in our efforts, I stand before you as chief executive of this state. And now—in keeping with the sanctioned privilege extended to all governors—it is my honor to address the people of this commonwealth and to express to my fellow citizens the profound gratitude and deep sense of purpose that I feel in fulfilling your expectations.

Candor and honesty would have me admit to you that I was not blessed with the foresight to know that this moment was in the offing when I stood here in 1985. Having been tested in the political crucible of trial and cross-examination, I have been rendered a verdict by having had delivered unto me the greatest outpouring of votes ever accorded any candidate for this great office. For that, I shall be eternally grateful. And—be assured—I shall demonstrate that gratitude during the next four years by being a governor who will be beholden to but one special interest: the welfare of Virginians, all Virginians.

It is said, "To whom much is given, much shall be expected." I will be the first to admit that I have been the beneficiary of much through no endeavors of my own. While I have indeed worked hard and performed to the best of my abilities, I have also had a few breaks along the way.

Indeed, in every walk—in every period of my life—there have been many more deserving and justly entitled to the fruits that wholesome opportunities present. And yet, for many, those chances never came, and the bell of fulfillment never tolled for them. Providence, indeed, has directed my course. And I shall remain ever mindful of my good fortune.

At this time—and in the place where so many great names in American history have trod—we renew this celebration of freedom in the full and certain knowledge that with it comes great responsibility.

. . .

Without question, much tighter economic times which loom in the days ahead will test to the fullest our ability to make hard decisions, to lead, and to govern. But progress will be possible. Opportunity can be expanded.

Freedom can be increased.

Resources employed in the past for the finer things in life can be—and will have to be—deployed for the more serious of our needs. For we know that freedom is but a word for the man or woman who needs and cannot find a job.

Freedom—as it has been written—is a dream deferred when it "dries up like a raisin in the sun and stinks like rotten meat."

Freedom is meaningless when a woman's right to choose is regulated outside the dictates of her own faith and conscience.

Freedom is impotent when there is intolerance to those who hold moral and political beliefs different from our own.

Freedom is restricted when labor and management cannot reach agreements.

Freedom is impossible for the uneducated who try to live in today's complex world.

Freedom is restrained for business and industry when our network of transportation is allowed to deteriorate.

Freedom for the police is denied when their resources are unduly limited.

Freedom for the people is assaulted when lawful authority is abused.

Freedom for the next generation is mortgaged when we destroy our environment.

And—as has been proven throughout recorded history—freedom is nowhere to be found when the people are overtaxed and overregulated.

As we salute the idea of freedom today, let us pledge to extend that same freedom to others tomorrow. Let us fulfill the perfect promise of freedom and liberty left as a legacy for us by those who founded this commonwealth.

And let us likewise be thankful that—while our country gave birth to a freedom long denied and delayed for all who loved freedom—the

belief in these dreams held by those forebears was passed from genera-
tion to generation and spawned the seeds that propagated the will and
the desire to achieve.

We are on hallowed ground today, and the steps we take from
this place must be steps of honor. The words we issue must be words of
wisdom. The laws we pass must be laws of mercy and justice. And the
faith we possess must be true to the Almighty.

I paused at the end to raise my hands in a gesture of welcome and celebration. The crowd was with me, and I know I was grinning from ear to ear. I also knew that the moment wasn't a fulfillment of my journey but the hard-won beginning. Now it was time to govern.

I was elated with my victory, sober about the depth and breadth of the responsibility, and conscious of my historic obligation. But I was also wide-eyed and clear about remaining true to myself. Within weeks of my election, I received two letters addressed to "The Honorable L. Douglas Wilder." The first was from the Country Club of Virginia: "I am pleased to . . . extend to you an invitation to become an Honorary Member of the Country Club *during the term of your office as Governor of Virginia*" (emphasis added). The second letter was from the president of the Commonwealth Club, who wrote, "My fervent hope is that you will accept our invitation to membership." I never accepted their invitations to join. I didn't want the criteria for the acceptance of the first African American member to be misconstrued to mean that you had to first be the governor. I didn't want to be a member of any club that would single me out but refuse African American membership. And although I turned them down, I soon thereafter recommended the names of other African Americans who were admitted to the clubs. It was an interesting moment, but I didn't pay it much mind. I had work to do.

CHAPTER SEVEN

In the Saddle

As INSPIRING AND HISTORIC AS THE INAUGURATION WAS, IT SURPRISED me how many people became indifferent after the fact, as if the only point was achieving the winning vote count. Even today, the biographies of me contain little detail after the 1989 election. The election itself was enough for most people. But I didn't run for governor to be a historic totem. I ran because I wanted to get things done. And that required me to make decisions that inevitably disappointed my rosy-eyed supporters. Decades later, I would see a parallel in Barack Obama's experience. His inauguration day, like mine, was an ecstatic triumph, the capital a sea of tear-streaked faces, many of them African American, witnessing his historic oath. But the drama of a new day soon fell away to the practical realities of governing, and once he took his seat in the Oval Office, President Obama transitioned from being an emblem of hope to a controversial administrator of a divided country.

As I began my term, I was well aware that the high expectations of some and the low expectations of others would lead to intense scrutiny over every move I made. I would be immediately tested. I knew that my chief responsibility as governor was to stabilize the state's economy, which meant making hard choices, bound to be unpopular on both sides of the aisle. The economy was headed into a recession, and our state was facing the same crisis as the rest of the nation, enhanced by some special problems of our own.

I have a favorite quote from Ralph Waldo Emerson: "Events are in the saddle, and they ride mankind." The truth of this became clear to me before I'd even taken office. I arrived at the governor's office the week before Christmas, accompanied by Paul Goldman, for a twenty-minute briefing on the state budget. I had been pressing for this meeting ever since this election, and this was it—a short meeting crowded into the busy Christmas schedule. Governor Baliles told me, "I'm not going to leave you broke, but I'm not going to leave you with much." I asked, "How much?" and he replied, "Thirty-five million dollars."

"Good Lord." I was stunned. I asked if I could see the proposed budget and compare it with what I had understood. He stalled, telling me that he wanted to get it to the Speaker of the House and he had not finished it. He was saying, in effect, that there was no deficit that merited my concern. (As a result of Governor Baliles's failure to inform me of the budget situation in a timely manner, in my term, the legislature obligated the governor to notify the new governor of the state of the budget by early December. I welcomed the change but had already vowed to do just that for my successor.)

This was my inaugural present. I felt weak at the knees. Right away, I knew I would have to run an exceptionally lean government and do something to build a rainy-day fund—and do it all without raising taxes. I wouldn't be getting a honeymoon.

Virginia has long been known as a fiscally conservative state, and that has been a mostly accurate depiction. However, during prosperous times, even the most conservative politicians tend to release their grip on funds, buoyed by the combination of money in the till and the public clamor for more services. No one likes to make tough choices, and in good times, there is a myth that you don't have to. More gets spent, and less gets saved—the situation I found myself in when I began my term.

Since I was a Democrat and an African American, many people assumed that I was on the side of spending, but being tightfisted was in my blood. I'd never shaken the basic homeschooling I'd received coming up in a family where not a penny was wasted. My parents were masters at making a dollar out of fifteen cents, and the lesson stuck with me. So I followed my instincts during those early days as governor and began the process of rightsizing Virginia's budget. We funded necessities over niceties, and we avoided increasing taxes. The people of Virginia were hurting economically, and I wasn't about to lead the charge to have their dreams dashed and their financial house collapse because government decided to spend more and more.

In my first State of the Commonwealth address, shortly after my inauguration, I outlined three key principles:

1. To resist the urge to enact general tax increases

2. To refrain from increasing total appropriations

3. To establish an unobligated reserve in the biennial budget

Out of necessity, it was a fiscally conservative approach. I quoted President John F. Kennedy's first State of the Union address, in which he said, "To state the facts frankly is not to despair the future nor indict the past. The prudent heir takes careful inventory of his legacies and gives a faithful accounting to those whom he owes an obligation of trust." One of my Republican colleagues said it was the best *Republican* speech he'd ever heard a Democrat utter. Many of my supporters and detractors were surprised to wake up and find they had elected a governor with an austerity platform. The budget was revamped, and a rainy-day fund was created and put into the state constitution. At the same time, while managing the fiscal crisis, I was determined not to shortchange the people and to preserve the programs that were important to their welfare.

My first year as governor was a whirlwind of activity, just the way I liked it. Of course, as a single man in the governor's house, I was a curiosity, and my personal life was a topic of ongoing speculation. My daughter, Lynn, who was in her late twenties, lived in the adjoining mansion facilities, as Baliles's son had done. She often filled in as the hostess at state dinners. She relished the role, and I was proud of her ability to easily mix with world and national leaders. I never felt lessened by the absence of a proper First Lady by my side.

However, the media (like nature) abhors a vacuum, so the rumors about my relationship with Patricia Kluge began hitting the gossip columns. Patricia and her husband, billionaire John Kluge, had been early supporters of mine during my run for governor, and we'd become close friends. John and Patricia were among the first to believe in me, and I never forgot that. When the Kluges announced that they would be divorcing during the first year of my term, the speculation immediately began that Patricia and I had a relationship. Reporters eagerly followed the trail, looking for sightings. One of the jokes that often surfaced referred to my taking many helicopter rides to see her. I always found it amazing that with all the speculation, the press never managed to produce a photograph of me taking a helicopter to visit Patricia or showed us together on or near a helicopter.

The truth about my bachelorhood was far less interesting than the speculation. I was basically married to my job, with very limited private time to myself. Faced with a choice between pursuing a serious relationship or remarriage and being fully immersed in public life, I chose the latter. I didn't want to repeat the mistakes I'd made during my marriage, when I was so wrapped up in my work that I failed to be an attentive husband. If anything, my work was more demanding than ever. I also had the capacity to be content with myself, something that remains true. My social life has always been active, but in the end, I never considered remarrying. As governor, I had plenty to occupy myself. There was never a day that I didn't wake up with a full plate of challenges. On the good days, those challenges were about governing the state of Virginia. On the bad days, they were about distracting political annoyances that took far more time, energy, and emotional resources than they deserved.

Chuck Robb and I had long ago made our peace for the good of the party and the state, but our uneasy pact threatened to blow apart in a very public way. It began in the spring of 1991 during a tough period for Robb.

There had been a number of public embarrassments in his private life, including the statement by a former Miss Virginia that she'd had an affair with him while he was governor. There were also allegations that Robb had attended parties where cocaine was being used. What made this episode difficult for me was Robb's contention that I had ordered state police to look into his personal life. I couldn't imagine what he was talking about until it was revealed that he'd listened to tapes of confidential calls I had made on the phone in my state car, referring to Robb's personal troubles.

That's how I learned that I had been wiretapped by someone probably close to Robb, if not on his staff. I was traveling in Europe on a trade mission when the news broke about the tapes. I was furious. "It's wiretapping, and it's a criminal act," I told the media, chilled by the revelation that a governor's most private interactions could be tape-recorded and disseminated to the public. Robb's spokesman immediately put out a statement: "Neither Senator Robb nor anyone on his staff has been involved in providing tapes to anyone or playing such tapes for Democrats. Senator Robb has never heard tapes of this type."

This denial turned out to be not exactly true. Investigators never found Robb's fingerprints on the tapes, although he later admitted to having been aware of their existence. Several people told me that Robb had received the tapes, and when reporters asked me if Robb was behind the circulation of the tapes, I said yes. Privately, I had no idea, but the whole matter seemed characteristic of the thin-skinned attitudes I'd encountered before with Robb. Those attitudes have a way of trickling down to the staff level, so although Robb might not have instigated the taping, loyal staffers could have thought they had carte blanche. Perhaps they were worried that I had damaging information about Robb. I honestly don't know what the wiretappers were looking for.

There was no doubt in my mind that there existed in Robb's office and among his supporters an atmosphere of disdain for me and my administration that spilled over into illegal acts. Among Robb's closest aides were those intent on my destruction. This was confirmed well into the wiretapping investigation when the *Virginian-Pilot* published a memorandum written in 1991 by an aide to Robb. The memo was thick with vitriol, accusing me, Paul Goldman, and my chief of staff, Jay Shropshire, of being "vindictive, petty, untrustworthy, devious, and that they will lie to your face, spread scurrilous rumors, and use any tactics of intimidation and threat they feel are necessary for their purposes." Wondering how to strategically deal with such people, Christine Bridge asked, "Do we maintain a civil distance from him as a public figure but continue to use sarcasm, undercurrents of information to reporters, and personal comments to define our disdain for him and his staff?"

When the embarrassing memo was made public, I was disgusted. I was in no mood to be conciliatory when Robb tried to clean up the mess. He called to tell me that an apology was on its way to me from Bridge, but when it was hand delivered by a messenger, I sent it back unopened. Instead, I decided to call a press conference in Washington to give an open airing to the mess. Robb urged me to stay silent, saying to make the issue more public would only hurt the party. But I refused. Standing before the Washington press corps, I said, "The whole sordid affair of illegal distribution of an illegally made tape recording, misappropriated federal campaign funds, the use of Democratic Senate Campaign Committee staff to discredit a sitting Democratic governor, and the spreading of scurrilous lies has not been seen in this country since Watergate."

The effort to get to the bottom of the matter would involve a year-long federal investigation. Eventually, three Robb aides pleaded guilty to secretly tapping my phone and then engaging in a conspiracy. David McCloud's testimony was particularly damning, leaving no doubt that the scheme had been an effort to discredit me. Once again, Robb and I had an uncomfortable meeting. He told me, "We both had people around us that didn't serve us well." We left it at that, but we continued to have an uneasy relationship.

Mostly, I was disappointed. So was the public, and Robb's future reelection seemed to be in jeopardy. A Mason-Dixon poll conducted in June 1992 found that Robb's approval ratings suffered from the scandals to the extent that he would lose a reelection fight if I, Coleman, Trible, or Oliver North were his opponent.

People often joke about politics being a dirty game, and many of them relish the mudslinging. I've never thought of politics as a game at all, and I reject the idea that you have to sling mud to come out on top. I'd like to state categorically what I've stated publicly before. Notwithstanding what may have occurred between us during that rough spot in our political lives, I credit Robb with being forward thinking enough to inspire a change in Virginia and the Democratic Party that allowed many progressive Democrats to win elections in the last three decades.

—~—

I tried not to let the wiretapping investigation distract me, and months into the investigation, I announced that I was running for president. People have often puzzled over my decision to announce a candidacy for president less than two years into my term as governor. I don't see why. There's no reason why I shouldn't have been a candidate. Few people run for the highest office in the land out of retirement. Most are from the ranks of statehouses and Congress; as I write this, the 2016 slates are coming together, with several acting governors forming exploratory commissions. During the 1992 campaign, Bill Clinton, who would of course win the presidency, was the sitting governor of Arkansas. But for some reason, my announcement generated a lot of scorn and disbelief. I don't think I'm being overly sensitive when I suggest that I was being judged by a different standard.

In reality, I had discovered that being a governor meant being irrevocably tied to the activities of Washington. I was frustrated to find that the budding opportunities in my state were increasingly blocked by the growing fiscal mess that consumed more and more of our limited resources to pay for Washington's fiscal follies. Washington's mismanagement was pushing Virginia into its worst budget crunch in forty years.

I fought cynicism about Washington but felt a growing sense of indignation. I was fed up with the deal making in Washington—from both parties—whose effects trickled down to the states. Yes, we had a two-party system: the Party Inside making the deals and the Party Outside, the rest of us, suffering as a result.

I was also deeply troubled by the deterioration in race relations. For the first time in fifty years, we seemed to be going backward because some leaders were pitting Americans against each other over the phony issue of racial quotas. It was morally unsupportable and fiscally irresponsible. If Bush's troubled economy created suffering over jobs and opportunities, it wasn't because of so-called racial quotas. But it was a convenient excuse for people who needed a scapegoat.

I was particularly incensed when Bush caved to the wishes of Senator Jesse Helms of North Carolina and vetoed the Civil Rights Act of 1990, which was designed to prevent discrimination in hiring. Helms had made the bill the centerpiece of his successful reelection campaign against Harvey Gantt, the African American mayor of Charlotte. In one particularly horrific television ad, a pair of white hands were shown crumpling a job rejection letter while a grim voice-over sympathized, "You needed that job, and you were the best qualified, but they had to give it to a minority because of a racial quota. Is that really fair? Harvey Gantt says it is."

President Bush had originally been in favor of the bill, but his tune changed after the election, as the Helms crowd made it clear that he couldn't hope to win reelection if he abandoned southern whites. I expressed my dismay in a strongly worded letter to the president:

"By falsely characterizing the Civil Rights Act of 1990 as a law requiring racial quotas, you laid the groundwork for Sen. Helms to raise the phony issue of racial quotas. After the election, you refused to condemn the Helms campaign's use of intimidation tactics against minority voters. The White House has abdicated its responsibility by serving as the leading apologist for the unconscionable actions of Sen. Jesse Helms."

There's no question that this incident tipped the scale in my deciding to run for president. I met with friends and advisers in a packed room to discuss the possibility. Everyone agreed that Washington was broken. The question was whether or not we could make a critical impact. "A southern governor can win," I said, knowing it to be true.

I threw my hat into the 1992 presidential race on September 14, 1991, at a time when President Bush might have seemed invincible. Bush had been very popular after the Gulf War, but the Democrats saw an opening in the struggling economy—not to mention the "law of twelve," or the tendency of voters to choose a different party after one had dominated the White House for more than eight years.

Speaking directly to Virginians, I explained why as their governor I felt compelled to take this step:

Twenty months ago, I committed and promised Virginians that I would work to solve the pressing problems of Virginia and position Virginia for the future. I will not shirk from that commitment one iota nor fall short on my promise one scintilla. In seeking the presidency, I recognize that I am the longest of long shots. I may not win. I may not get but a few votes.

But I would not be doing my job as governor—indeed, I would not deserve to be who I am—if I failed to step forward at this critical juncture in our nation's history.

The economy was much on my mind. But so was the fearsome specter of retreat on racial progress, and I addressed that as well:

When was the last time we had a president of the United States who went out of his way to raise the phony and divisive issue of racial quotas in hopes of turning back the clock on civil rights? Ever since Franklin Roosevelt, America has always had a president who understood that it was his self-evident obligation to lead America in this area—a responsibility which is not merely a matter of policy but a matter of morality, humanity, and eternal justice. Truman answered the call. Eisenhower answered. Kennedy answered. Johnson took the clarion firmly in hand. Nixon heard and answered the call. Ford did his duty . . . even Ronald Reagan was forced to heed that call. But not George Bush. For the first time in a great many years, the president of the United States is leading the retreat. Instead of healing leadership, he offers divisive rhetoric that can only result in pitting one group of Americans against another.

It was a little more than a year before the election. At that time, the length of the presidential primary season was still manageable. When I announced, I was among the first. Governor Clinton was said to be considering a run but had not yet announced a candidacy. My announcement also positioned me as a national centrist, a shift away from the Jesse Jackson wing of the party. Jackson had become a perennial presidential candidate and now was mulling a third run.

Evaluating the role of African American politicians in presidential campaigns, journalist Mary McCrory captured the shift, writing in the *Washington Post*, "To Democrats, Wilder represents the hope that they may one day soon escape from the Jackson bondage. . . . Jackson, a towering, lowering presence, fills many Democrats with apprehension. In two presidential campaigns he has proved implacable. Wilder, of medium height, with silky white hair and amiable mien, they find infinitely reassuring. . . . Wilder does not presume to speak for black people. He presents himself as a success story who happens to be black. The sense of grievance that Jackson presents is absent."

Among the contenders on the Democratic side, in addition to Clinton, were former senator Paul Tsongus, Senator Tom Harkin, Senator Bob Kerrey, former governor Jerry Brown, and former senator Eugene McCarthy.

My decision to seek the presidential nomination was not especially popular at home, but I had my convictions. I was compelled to give it a try, to see if my message would resonate on a larger scale. I saw that my very presence in the race shifted the conversation to the issues I cared about. In speeches across the country, I spoke of a "New Mainstream"— fiscally conservative, socially progressive, and grounded in pragmatism.

In this way, my candidacy helped shift the party toward the center. As a "new" African American politician, I transcended the traditional polarizing tracts on race that had been a hallmark of previous contenders like Jackson. It was the same approach that would prove successful for Barack Obama sixteen years later. But the awakening came too late for me.

In New Hampshire, before a single primary vote was cast, I was slammed up against the cold reality of race. My campaign had put together several focus groups to test my positions with voters. The result was shocking. *Chicago Tribune* writer Clarence Page later described one of the focus groups:

> *New Hampshire voters liked what they heard, but not as it turned out, what they saw. They liked what they heard about Wilder's fiscal conservatism, his balancing his state budget and his medal-winning Korean War combat exploits.*
>
> *But when a biographical video was played and they saw the candidate for the first time, the mood noticeably changed from joy to chagrin. In one eyebrow-raising outburst, a surprised woman told the woman sitting next to her, "He's black!" It wasn't that they were antiblack, they said. Rather, "My neighbors probably wouldn't like it" or "I don't think New Hampshire will go for that."*

The experience was repeated in other focus groups. That poor early showing, combined with the unpopularity of my run among Virginians and the demands of my office, convinced me to leave the race. Running for our nation's highest office was a full-time job, and I was not willing to put aside a job as governor that I loved dearly.

At my State of the State address to the General Assembly, I announced my decision. "Long before I announced for president, I said that if it became too difficult for me to govern the commonwealth and conduct a presidential campaign, I would terminate one endeavor. I was left with a choice: either to devote all of my energies to delivering the message or to guiding Virginia through these difficult times. I have chosen the latter." I received the largest, heartiest cheer I'd ever heard from that body. It was obviously the right thing to do. In retrospect, I can see that my run for president hurt my standing with Virginia voters. The polls were evidence of their displeasure, and I accept that. The people spoke.

With my withdrawal from the race, the question became which candidate I would back. By most political calculations, the African American vote was now in play, and my endorsement was worth something. I was circumspect, though—not really ready to make a choice. Senator Bob Kerrey as good as promised me the vice president's slot if he were nominated—not that I was interested. When Ross Perot decided to run as an Independent, his campaign had conversations with Paul Goldman about the possibility of my being his running mate. News of this courting didn't sit well with my fellow Democrats, especially Bill Clinton, who was emerging as the front-runner. As the nominating convention at Madison Square Garden in New York City approached, my failure to endorse Clinton, the presumptive nominee, was causing heartburn in the party. I fielded numerous calls from Ron Brown, the Democratic National Committee chairman, and I was being roundly criticized for staying silent, although others, like Mario Cuomo and Jesse Jackson, had not yet endorsed Clinton. I refused to be pressured. When I finally did endorse him the week before the convention, I also secured a speaking spot. This was very important to me. I had things to say, and I was eager to say them. Standing before the convention, I spoke with great passion about the failures of President Bush and the dream we longed to recapture:

> George Bush has not led America forward. Sadly, he has led us in circles, and sometimes setting the clock back on our progress. The Bush administration has failed, and not just because George Bush is too liberal or too conservative. Rather, it's been a question of trust. George Bush may be willing to do whatever it takes to win again. And when he was asked as to why he deserved another term as president of the United States, he said, "That's the same question Barbara asked me this morning." And his answer: "We've got to finish what we started."

Well, what did he start? Nothing. And what did he finish? Nothing. . . . Our freedom at home is at risk; an economy stifled by debt and policies that reward the privileged few. For the last dozen years, the Republicans have had their trickle-down; nothing new has been trickling down ever since Warren G. Harding. We're not going to have that in our country, because we're going to elect our people at the statehouse, at the courthouse, but the most important thing, we're going to elect Bill Clinton and Al Gore to the White House, 1992.

My heart was particularly full in those days with a sense of historic promise long denied. Shortly before the convention, I had returned from a historic and meaningful twenty-three-day trade mission to sub-Saharan Africa, believing that we were bound by a common struggle against oppression and toward prosperity and human rights. I had long felt this connection. One of my first directives as governor had been to bar state agencies and universities from investing in companies that did business with the apartheid nations of South Africa. I also had the honor of forming a relationship with Nelson Mandela, one of the most remarkable men I have ever met. What impressed me most about him was his complete lack of bitterness or recrimination. He radiated a positive spirit that was both inspiring and effective in his quest to end apartheid.

It so happened that both Mandela and I were in New York City during convention week—he to speak at the United Nations. We met together for an hour, and as always, I drew strength from Mandela's unwavering determination and his warm personality. In the company of Mandela, anything seemed possible. It was clear to me that he would have fit quite comfortably at a table talking with the greatest Virginians. He knew not only how to demand liberty with eloquence but also how to turn it into a reality. Not many are born with the talent to do both. President Mandela and I shared a deep and abiding faith in the people: The people are always ready for change, they hunger for change, and, if given a chance, they will always rise to the occasion.

———

For me, leadership was often about being decisive in situations that were not cut and dried. It meant shutting out the rhetoric and learning the facts and then acting. I cannot think of a single pressing issue facing Virginia that was a slam dunk. The nuances of governing existed below the headlines—a truth I had lived throughout my political career. I tried to be mindful of the words of Samuel Johnson: "Integrity without knowledge is weak and useless, and knowledge without integrity is dangerous and dreadful."

One of the most intellectually and morally difficult challenges to face me as governor involved the death penalty. During my term, there were fourteen executions by the electric chair, and every one of them required me to make a declaration.

I had campaigned on a strong law-and-order platform, including supporting the death penalty, but, frankly, few people believed I was sincere. Now my resolve would be examined in the light of my actions. For any governor, the death penalty is a test of both character and reason. Long after the verdict of death has been issued in a court of law and the appeals in the high courts have been exhausted, the final decision about whether the convict lives or dies is left to the governor. I did not relish this role, and I doubt that any of my peers in the statehouses do. However, I took my obligation with the utmost seriousness. For each death penalty case, I had the case files brought to my office, and I studied every piece of paper in an exhaustive effort to uncover a truth that could inform my decision. Having been a criminal trial lawyer for so many years, I knew the law. But this was a different obligation.

Perhaps the most high-profile case I had to make a decision about involved a man named Roger Keith Coleman, a coal miner who had received the death penalty for the 1981 rape and fatal stabbing of his nineteen-year-old sister-in-law Wanda McCoy. Circumstantial evidence pointed to Coleman, and although this was before the use of DNA testing, there was blood-type and fingerprint evidence. He was convicted and sentenced to death in 1982.

During the appeals process, which went on for a decade, Coleman consistently denied his guilt, and his death sentence was a cause célèbre in the anti–death penalty movement. While in prison, he gave many interviews and received global support for his cause. *Time* magazine published a cover story days before the scheduled execution titled "This Man Might Be Innocent." Coleman became a celebrity, giving interviews from death row to Larry King, Phil Donahue, the *Today* show, and *Good Morning America*. I received more than 13,000 letters urging clemency.

But in spite of Coleman's public relations push, the evidence against him actually grew stronger over the years. Inexplicably, his defense team introduced the results of genetic tests in 1990 that showed Coleman to be among 0.2 percent of the population who could have raped McCoy. Furthermore, Coleman demanded and was given a last-minute lie detector test that he failed. In reviewing the case, I found the evidence persuasive, and on May 19, 1992, with appeals exhausted, I announced that I would not intervene. The next day, Coleman was executed in the electric chair. His last words before he died were a declaration of his innocence: "An innocent man is going to be murdered tonight. When my innocence is proven, I hope Americans will realize the injustice of the death penalty as all other civilized countries have."

Many people persisted in the belief that the state of Virginia executed an innocent man. I remember one woman in particular who interviewed me in Richmond and angrily accused me of allowing Coleman's execution as a way of proving my conservative credentials. In the following years, Coleman was often used as a poster boy for the anti–death penalty movement. But there is a dramatic twist to the story. In 2006, Governor Mark Warner ordered DNA testing of the initial evidence. It was a match with Coleman, with only a one-in-19-million chance that the DNA was not his.

I didn't learn of the retesting until after the fact and would have appreciated a call from Warner's office. I thought the protocol, especially the ethos in Virginia, would have demanded that—not to mention that I had contributed more to Warner being elected than almost anyone. I was well aware that a negative result would have put me in the spotlight for having allowed an innocent man to be sent to his death. There was no reaction on my part, as I knew I had been justified.

Another death penalty case, involving a man named Earl Washington, demonstrates the difficulty of getting to the full truth in the time before DNA testing was available. Washington was accused of the 1982 rape and murder of Rebecca Lynn Williams, a nineteen-year-old mother of three. Washington, who had a low IQ of around sixty-nine, came to the attention of authorities a year after the murder when he was arrested for burglary in another county. After two days of questioning, police announced that he had confessed to several crimes, including Williams's murder. His interview was awash with red flags suggesting that Washington was not the killer. He did not know the race of his victim or the address of the apartment where she was killed or that he had raped her—among other discrepancies. The police rehearsed the testimony several times before they had him sign the confession. As the Innocence Project would later detail, there were many problems with the prosecution of Washington that indicated he was being railroaded. Nevertheless, he was convicted and sentenced to death based almost entirely on his confession.

In 1993, DNA testing was done on the semen stain found at the scene, and Washington was excluded as a contributor. It had little effect because Virginia's arcane law allowed defendants only twenty-one days to introduce new evidence, and he'd missed the deadline! I knew I had to act. Days before I left office, I commuted Washington's sentence to life imprisonment. In 2000, Governor Gilmore ordered additional DNA testing, which proved conclusive, and Gilmore ordered an absolute pardon, clearing Washington of the murder charges. When he was released in early 2001, he had spent eighteen years in prison, half of it on death row, for a crime he did not commit. In 2007, Kenneth M. Tinsley, who was serving life in prison for a 1984 rape, pleaded guilty to Williams's rape and murder and was sentenced to two additional life terms.

With the state-of-the-art use of DNA evidence in the courtroom, it becomes less likely that people like Washington will be railroaded this way. But there is also an issue of prosecutorial integrity. Even without DNA proof, Washington should never have been brought to trial. The desperation to get a conviction—any conviction—was the result of an overly zealous prosecutor. The quest for "law and order" is hollow if we knowingly convict innocent people.

My law-and-order stance also involved guns. Virginia was known to be a source of gun trafficking. Federal authorities dubbed Interstate 95 from Virginia to New York the "Iron Corridor" because of the guns flowing north through our state. In 1991, the Bureau of Alcohol, Tobacco, and Firearms found that 40 percent of the 1,236 guns found at crime scenes in New York had been purchased in Virginia. Often, the gun traffickers paid ordinary citizens to make multiple purchases—so-called straw purchases—thus covering their tracks.

In 1993, I proposed a law that would limit handgun purchases to one a month, a move that was immediately slammed by the National Rifle Association but succeeded in spite of intense pro-gun lobbying. It was notable that my one-handgun-a-month law passed in Virginia, a state where gun ownership was sacrosanct. I convinced the public that I was not against guns—I owned one myself and had hunted pheasants. When I asked the opponents, "How does limiting handgun purchases to twelve a year infringe on your rights?" the only response was the old "slippery slope" argument—that any limitation opened the door to taking guns away altogether. This argument is still used today, regardless of the absence of any evidence. I have never heard a public official call for the removal of all handguns! I've never understood this argument. We place restrictions on other individual rights in order to protect the public good. What's so special about guns? Besides, my one-handgun-a-month law made practical sense. "How many guns do you need?" I asked—a question that would be considered heretical in today's pro-gun climate.

My effort to restrict handgun purchases was aided by the fact that it was, relatively speaking, a golden age of gun control. The Brady Bill passed that year with support from both houses of Congress, and the nation as a whole was favorably disposed to gun control.

As a sad commentary on how our national conversation about guns has deteriorated, Governor Bob McDonnell signed a measure to repeal the law in 2012 after it passed in the state senate by one vote. (John Edwards and Creigh Deeds were the only Democrats to vote for the measure.) By that point, many politicians were scared silly to be seen opposing the National Rifle Association, and it's only getting worse.

———

During my four years as governor, I got things done. My mantra was to be socially progressive and fiscally conservative. New faces were appointed to significant positions across Virginia. Coalitions were built across party lines in the General Assembly. Under my leadership, Virginia's government became more diverse. For the first time in the state's history, two African Americans and two women served in the cabinet, and during my term, thirty-four African Americans and forty-six women were in charge of state agencies and departments. Diversity, I believed, was the signature of prosperity.

My greatest achievement was getting the state on its feet financially.

Virginia was one of only two states at that time to address a budget shortfall without raising taxes. *Financial World* magazine rated Virginia the best-managed state twice during my term. The irony was clear. My opponents, along with some in the media, liked to portray me as a "tax-and-spend liberal" because that's just what you said about Democrats. But in my case, it was far from the truth. My policy chief, Mac MacFarlane, once said of me, "He'd squeeze a Buffalo nickel until you see it crap on the floor." *That* was the truth.

If financial stability and economic progress were the hallmarks of my tenancy in the governor's office, one defeat was the greatest personal and professional disappointment of my term—the failure to bring the Washington Redskins to Virginia. In 1992, after much wooing, the Redskins owner, Jack Kent Cooke, and I reached an initial agreement to build a new stadium for the Redskins at the Potomac Yards in Alexandria. I presented the plan to the legislature and considered it a great opportunity.

The state would take on what I thought was a modest $130 million share of the $280 million project.

I was disappointed when news of the plan unleashed a huge public backlash, especially among Northern Virginians. The plan was clobbered in the polls and among legislators, who felt they had been left out of the dialogue and taken for granted. Cooke had insisted, over my objections, that he didn't want anyone outside my administration involved in the discussions and that all negotiations were to be confidential.

The way I saw it, the stadium proposal was a vehicle of prosperity and would have greatly benefited the economy of Virginia, especially the north. In the end, it never happened, and Potomac Yards is still Potomac Yards. The combination of the stadium's unpopularity and Cooke's dogmatism scuttled the deal. Yet it's hard to find anyone today who admits to having opposed the project.

The stadium fight was bruising, but I believed in it. I kept my own conscience and was not swayed by political calculations that did not serve a higher purpose. The reporter Margaret Edds once described my administration in the context of something her ten-year-old son said to her: "You are not the boss of me."

It was true. I was stubborn, I knew my own mind, and I was focused on my goals. As I had done throughout my political career, I always tried to look at what the issues were and administrate fairly. Whether the topic was affordable housing or health care or education, the goal was always to lift up those who lacked opportunity and provide a better life for all regardless of race. I knew that there were those who worried about me catering to African Americans, but I was never fearful about this charge because it was never true. Equality was essential to good government, and that meant everyone got a fair share of the pie—from the poor miners in western Virginia to the disadvantaged people of the urban centers.

The quality that guided my life and work was never being satisfied, never resting, never believing I'd achieved success. Success is not achieved; it's something you continue to work at. From childhood, I'd been urged to develop the highest possibility of my potential, and that meant there would never be an end point, a time to relax and coast. I occupied a limited time and space on earth, and I was always asking what more I could do with it.

As I neared the end of my term, my thoughts turned to my successor. My favored successor was Mary Sue Terry, who had earned her stripes serving two terms as attorney general. I told her that I was very much interested in her succeeding me and that I'd do everything I could to help her. But she was overly skittish about taking my advice or utilizing my support. I was concerned. Terry was easily nominated by the Democrats, but she was facing a formidable candidate in George Allen, the son of a popular football coach. Allen was a bright guy who, although he was born in California, had perfected an easygoing "ol' boy" southern charisma.

My analysis was that Allen would be a tough candidate to beat, but Terry simply didn't believe it. In June, she was up in the polls by twenty-nine points, and she planned to ride out that lead. I made numerous efforts to warn her about the tidal wave that was about to hit her campaign, to no avail.

The way I viewed it, Terry got that lead from me; voters were generally happy with my administration. But you don't win elections because voters are happy with someone else. You win them on your own, and eventually, when voters began evaluating their choice, Terry's lead evaporated.

There was no denying that the two candidates presented a sharp contrast that didn't favor Terry. Allen was a talented politician, with a strong campaign team and a winning grassroots manner. Voters like to see that politicians enjoy the ride, and Allen certainly did. Terry, on the other hand, seemed to find campaigning a grind, and it showed. She never provided voters with a face they'd want representing their state for four years. A simple truth was becoming clear: Voters look for something different in an attorney general than they do in a governor. Terry never captured that appeal.

As Larry Sabato wrote, Terry ran an "inept" campaign. She squandered her lead with a campaign of entitlement, believing her past victories would give her a safe win. But the mood of an electorate isn't frozen in time. Its trust has to be earned in the present.

By September, Terry's lead had fallen to six points. I was preparing to go on a trade mission to China, and I offered to delay my trip to help with the campaign. Terry refused my offer. She assured me that she could handle it.

By the time I came back in October, Terry's margin had disappeared. Campaigning with her in black churches, I witnessed her struggling to define herself. I remember one woman asking her why she was running. She replied by saying she wanted to take my place. The woman calmly told her, "Yes, we're all proud of the governor, but I'm not asking about him. Tell me about yourself and why I should vote for *you*." Terry never could give this voter a reason why she deserved her vote. It was painful to watch.

In addition, Terry's indifference disappointed me. Recalling how blindsided I'd been by the fiscal situation I faced upon election, I decided to invite Terry and Allen in for a budget briefing in September, months before the election, so they'd have all the facts on hand. Terry came alone, which surprised me since I had never known her to be a fiscal wonk. She said she was pleased to have an opportunity to vent with me and my fiscal staffs, though she asked few questions. Allen, however, arrived with his entire team of financial advisers. They reviewed the documents, asked questions, and took copious notes.

By then, it was clear that Terry was outmatched. Allen won the election in a landslide, aided by strong contingents from the newly empowered Christian right. He also won the women's vote. Having failed to appeal to core constituencies, Terry received a lackluster showing in the African American community—something I might have helped her with had she been interested and had she been less contentious in her dealings with me. The attorney general is considered to be the governor's lawyer, yet Terry had sued me in three separate cases during my term, losing all three of them. She should have known that would hurt her with African Americans.

In office, Allen had many strong points, and he retained most of my staff. On the other hand, he attempted to unravel some of our advances and cater to the right of his party, with an agenda that focused on welfare reform, favored the oil and gun lobbies, and utilized some of the classic dog whistles of the old Byrd era. For three years running, Allen proclaimed April as Confederate History and Heritage Month. He refused to use the term "Civil War," preferring to call it a "four-year struggle for independence and sovereign rights." Again, one step forward, two steps back.

<hr />

One of my final acts as governor was the conditional pardon of a young man named Allen Iverson, who was one of the most promising young basketball players in the country. (*USA Today* called him "the jewel" of college prospects.) Along with Iverson, I also pardoned two other youths who were convicted with him. It was a case that touched my heart for a very simple reason: the specter of African American youths being treated differently than others. In February 1993, Iverson, who was seventeen, and several of his friends had been involved in a dispute with some white youths at a bowling alley, and things got out of hand. During the brawl, Iverson allegedly hit a woman on the head with a chair. Police arrived and arrested Iverson and two of his friends but none of the white brawlers. Iverson was tried as an adult and convicted on the charge of maiming by a mob. (This charge was chilling given that the statute was originally introduced in response to lynching.) He was sentenced to fifteen years, with ten years suspended. He had been in prison for four months when I was asked to intercede and use the powers of the governor's office to correct an injustice.

In my mind, there was some doubt about the charge. Iverson and his friends hardly constituted a mob, and I felt it unfair that they were the only ones held to account. It seemed highly unusual that the young men were singled out for prosecution in this way. I didn't want to see young lives destroyed, so I gave them conditional clemency so that they could return to their homes and pursue their educations. An appeals court ultimately overturned the conviction, and Iverson went on to become a professional basketball star. Needless to say, my decision was not without controversy. The African American community was delighted, but others felt I was giving preferential treatment to Iverson and his friends because of their race. I saw it as righting an injustice and giving them a chance at life. I made no apologies for my choice.

As my term drew to an end, a *Richmond Times-Dispatch* editorial, "Wilder in Sum," reflected the spirit I tried to bring to the office. "Of our politicians we expect too much and move to knock them down no sooner than we raise them up. Doug Wilder ascended to power and lowered his shoulder into the prevailing winds. He presided never fearful of not being taken seriously by pseudos. He lived by the dictum that one never should be haughty to the humble—nor humble to the haughty. He recognized that when one is right no one remembers and when one is wrong no one forgets. And he prevailed."

In my last speech, before a crowd of three hundred, I presented a strong challenge to all elected officials and the people they serve:

> *We serve as role models, as keepers of the flame and symbols of what the people should strive for. When we go to a school and tell young children why they must stay away from drugs, we must have the moral authority to be trusted.*
>
> *Our young people today cannot be coddled or misled. They should not confuse the message. The African American community is beset with a lawlessness heretofore unknown. Notwithstanding any other contributing socioeconomic factors, those senseless crimes are wrong, and those who insist on breaking the law will and should be strictly punished. If it takes tough measures to deal with them, then that example should be set. Excuses and condoning must stop, and it should stop now.*

I addressed another matter of some interest in my remarks. Earlier in the year, I had flirted with the idea of running against Robb in the 1994

Senate race, but now I announced that I was withdrawing from consideration. Frankly, I didn't want to spend the next year immersed in brick throwing.

But it would not be the final word. Two months later, I changed course again after watching with dismay how Robb was becoming the butt of late-night television jokes, unable to shake the aura of personal and professional scandal. Some people were telling me I owed it to the state to enter the race and help restore Virginia's dignity in the eyes of the nation. We could do better. And then there was the matter of a man named Oliver North.

CHAPTER EIGHT

The Race Goes On

LARRY SABATO WOULD CALL IT "THE SENATE RACE FROM HELL." As the campaign season began for the 1994 Senate race, the pundits were in agreement that the scandal-wracked Robb was vulnerable. Even so, I had planned to stay out of the race. I left the governor's mansion with plenty of opportunities awaiting me, and I wasn't unhappy with the prospect of taking a break from politics. But when Lieutenant Colonel Oliver North emerged as the presumptive Republican candidate, the buzz from my supporters grew loud. Did these two men represent a choice that Virginia could stomach?

Oliver North's presence in the race was troubling. North had captivated the red-state imagination with his uber-patriotic stump speeches and right-wing swagger. He had stormed into the public view during the heated Iran-Contra hearings, and his conviction on sixteen felony counts (later vacated) served only to burnish his credentials. He came to be an emblem of the tough, take-no-prisoners soldier of the right, and for many people, his unapologetic attitude about his wrongdoings was appealing. He was a classic outsider, full of bluster with little in the way of governing substance. And not all Virginia Republicans embraced him. Well into the race, a group of them fronted an independent candidacy by none other than Marshall Coleman, a perennial candidate and my opponent in the 1989 election. He never made much impact.

And so I decided to return to the race as an Independent. The people of Virginia deserved a better choice. The Democrats were not happy with my decision. Even Vice President Al Gore invited me to the White House to persuade me not to challenge Robb. I politely declined.

On the ground, Robb and North tried to ignore Coleman and me and take swings at each other. It was an ugly campaign, focusing on character issues. I was personally dismayed when North, of all people, said that Robb had permanently alienated the African American community when his aides colluded in wiretapping me. At the same time, he argued that the Confederate flag was a symbol of the evils of slavery—a point of view I had not heard before and one that seemed disingenuous. Robb fought back, declaring, "My opponent is a document-shredding, Constitution-trashing, commander-in-chief-bashing, Ayatollah-loving, arms-dealing, criminal-protecting, résumé-enhancing, Noriega-coddling, Swiss-banking, lawbreaking, letter-faking, self-serving snake-oil salesman who can't tell the difference between the truth and a lie." And so it went.

At the beginning of September, entering the final stretch, we had a candidate debate. I was pleased to finally be sharing a stage with the others, and I made my independence clear. Noting that the two front-runners had made the campaign a referendum on character, I challenged both of them on that front.

Addressing North, I laid out some of his seedier associations during the Iran-Contra affair, wondering out loud what that said about his character. And I didn't let Robb off the hook. "You've been in the company of people who were convicted and sent away," I said to him. "And you were warned by your own attorney general to stay away, and you didn't. So don't tell me you're going to stand up on your moral horse now."

But soon after the debate, it became brutally clear that I had little chance of winning the seat, with poll numbers roughly half of Robb's and North's. I wasn't a fantasist. I realized that the ultimate effect of my name on the ballot would be to carve away at Robb's constituency enough to throw the election to North. This possibility was not lost on Washington. I was invited by the White House to meet with Vice President Al Gore and White House Chief of Staff Leon Panetta in Gore's office. The press got wind of the meeting and even went so far as to follow Gore's limo. We spoke about my leaving the race—something I had already decided to do. They offered to help with lingering campaign expenses. However, there was no quid pro quo. Had I stayed in the race, with the difficulties that Robb had encountered, North would almost certainly have been successful. I understood that splitting the Democratic vote could place the commonwealth and the country in a more perilous position than I could abide. My conscience would not allow me to be the cause of North's election. The consequences of that result went beyond the balance of power in the Senate. It would, I believed, be a shameful choice for Virginia. Withdrawing from the race, I said, "I am a realist. I know when to hold 'em and when to fold 'em."

I endorsed Robb with weeks to go and helped turn out the vote to defeat North, including an event with Robb and President Clinton in Fairfax that was very successful. Robb had reason to be overjoyed by my withdrawal. Experts later concluded that had I remained in the race, he would have lost the African American vote, which gave him the critical edge over North. After the election, Sabato wrote, "Had Wilder stayed in the race, he would surely have taken at least half of the black vote, or 130,000. Since Robb won the actual election by only 56,000 votes, the Democrat would have lost a Robb-North-Wilder-Coleman race by at least 74,000 votes, with North winning the Senate seat. That did not happen because Wilder not only dropped out of the contest but also endorsed his bitter rival enthusiastically. In the end, African American votes for Robb accounted for more than four times his margin of victory statewide."

Robb also benefited from the split that was becoming more apparent in the state of Virginia—between the more centrist "purple" north and the "red" south. Soon after I left the race, Robb and North engaged in a heated discussion of an old southern theme: the Confederate flag. North was quite open about his support for those who would display the flag, calling it "part of the great heritage" of Virginia and suggesting that those who opposed its display were beset by the scourge of political correctness. The flare-up didn't last long, but it was among a number of incidents when North displayed his deep red stripes.

Mainstream Republicans—even conservatives—had always been uncomfortable with North's candidacy. A case in point: A week before the election, no lesser figure than Nancy Reagan spoke out against him. Mrs. Reagan was appearing with Charlie Rose for a sit-down interview at the 92nd Street Y in New York City. When he asked her what she thought of North, she replied, "Ollie North? Oh, I'll be happy to tell you about Ollie North. Ollie North has a great deal of trouble separating fact from fantasy." As if that weren't bad enough, she went on to say, "He lied to my husband and lied about my husband. Kept things from him he should not have kept from him. And that's what I think of Ollie North."

Robb's ultimate victory over North, in a neck-and-neck election, was an outlier in 1994, as Republicans swept most seats, picking up eight Democratic seats and six open ones and taking control of the Senate. I believe that had the Republicans nominated a less scandal-tarred candidate and one more in tune with Virginia voters, Robb would have gone down too. Exit polls showed that four out of ten Robb votes were cast not *for* Robb but *against* North.

My next political role was not planned or expected. As we entered the new century, I was busy and content, teaching at Virginia Commonwealth University, working on a plan for a slavery museum, going out on my boat, and visiting with my grandchildren. A return to public life was not on my radar. In 2000, in his final year as senator and Clinton's as president, Chuck Robb called me and asked if I'd be interested in an appointment as judge for the U.S. Fourth Circuit Court of Appeals. He wanted to make a recommendation to President Clinton and said that with my experience, there wouldn't be any problem with confirmation. I thanked him but said, "Look, that isn't me. It's too sedentary. I can't see myself sitting all day." But I did suggest they take a look at my former law partner, Roger Gregory, who was very smart and capable. Robb recommended him, and Clinton nominated him.

It wasn't smooth sailing for Roger. At the time of his nomination, there were several other Clinton nominees being held up in the Senate, and the administration asked Roger if he would agree to a recess appointment. Roger and I talked it over and decided that would ring hollow. We wanted a full confirmation. I enlisted the aid of Senator John Warner, who was instrumental in getting Virginia's newest senator, former governor George Allen, on board. Allen reminded me recently that his speech on the Senate floor favoring Roger Gregory's nomination was the first of his terms. Allen also told me that the powerful senator Trent Lott had lobbied him to hold up Roger's nomination, and he'd refused. I was impressed to see Allen's display of political courage. Years later, when he lost his seat following the unfortunate "Macaca" incident, I felt that the characterization of him as a rube and a racist was completely unwarranted.

I was happy being on the sidelines. But events conspired to put me back in the saddle. I was growing increasingly troubled by conditions in my beleaguered city of Richmond, and I began speaking out about it, openly calling Richmond a cesspool of corruption and incompetence.

At the heart of this corrupt system was the unusual way the mayor was selected. Notice I say *selected*, not *elected*. Since 1948, the city charter had deemed that the mayor be chosen by the city council, not by the people of Richmond. And his role was that of a figurehead. The city manager technically ran the city. It was a system that didn't make any sense.

Richmond seemed to be crumbling in on itself; decay was all around us. The downtown was shabby, neighborhoods were in disrepair, the crime rate was rising, the schools were underperforming, and the infrastructure was trembling with age. The unemployment rate was hovering at an unsustainable 25 percent. It was a disgrace.

When I spoke out about it, I got plenty of push-back, but my words also rallied some like-minded people to my cause. One of these was my old Republican friend Tom Bliley, a former Richmond mayor and congressman. Tom and I decided to form a commission to look into how we might revive the city. The more we studied the matter, the clearer it became that if change were to come, we would have to completely undo the charter and place an *elected* mayor, not a city manager, at the helm.

This would not be an easy task. Changing the charter meant that first we had to get the city council to pass an ordinance requiring a referendum. The city council refused. We then had to resort to collecting enough signatures to put a referendum on the ballot and then convince Richmond residents to vote for it. There were a lot of opponents among the political establishment, including the current mayor, the Legislative Black Caucus, the Crusade for Voters (the largest African American political group), and just about every member of the legislature. The NAACP was against it, and the African American media vehemently opposed it. Their concern was that the change would create a throwback—that whites would take over and run everything and that African Americans would lose clout. To remedy this possibility, we included in the referendum a stipulation that to be elected, a candidate must win not only a majority of the vote citywide but also five of the nine districts, guaranteeing a fair vote spread.

We targeted 2003 for the ballot measure and enlisted Paul Goldman to lead the signature drive. We collected enough signatures, and on election day, the referendum passed with 80 percent of the vote. The result illustrated the truth of one of my favorite sayings: "The people are always ahead of the politicians." Change was in the air. The first mayoral election in fifty-six years would take place in 2004.

Now the task was to find the best candidate. I had a couple of people in mind. The first couldn't run because he had moved outside Richmond and lost his residency. The second was committed to another position. At this point, one of the businessmen involved in the process looked at me across a conference table and said, "You're going to have to do it."

That certainly wasn't my plan. "Give me a week," I said. "I'll find another candidate." But a week came and went, and back at the conference table, a groundswell began to form in favor of my running. In one sense, I think many people found it appealing that a person who was a symbol of making history would lead the city into a new era. But people also realized that I knew how to govern and that I could do so independently without being in the pocket of special interests.

At that point, I felt the weight of obligation mixed with the thrill of possibility settle in me. It was a familiar sensation. "Okay," I said. "I guess it's me."

Once I made the commitment, I enjoyed being back out on the stump, talking to the people. Their grievances were so pressing, their suffering so real. They loved their once-great city that had been left behind in almost every way. There wasn't a success story to be found in any public arena. The population was dwindling as the middle class fled in search of jobs, safety, opportunity, and better environments in which to raise their children. I spoke about cleaning house, about restoring promise, about making Richmond great again. I believed it could be done.

It was a crowded field. Also running were the current mayor, a local architect, and a member of the school board. Among them, I was the only one with substantial experience actually governing. On election day, I was swept to victory with 80 percent of the vote, and after ten years out of public office, at the age of seventy-three, I was back in the game.

The mood at my victory party, in the heart of downtown Richmond, was electric. I felt the energy of renewal all around me. "This is a new beginning," I told the crowd. "There is an opportunity for all of us to reach out and reclaim and rebuild. I want to see a Richmond that doesn't just have a post office address to designate us but rather a community that unites us."

In some respects, this was the biggest challenge of my career, although I had to chuckle when my daughter related my eldest grandson's take on the matter. He'd asked, "Didn't you say that granddaddy has been a senator, a lieutenant governor, and then governor? Isn't he going backwards?"

From the start, I had to tackle a city bureaucracy that simply wasn't functional. Departments were badly coordinated and duplicating efforts, money was flowing down a drain of inefficiency, and we were paying far more than the going rate for contracts and services. Outsourcing in the housing and utilities departments was costing millions of dollars more than it would if we handled it on the inside. The retirement system was on shaky ground. As mayor, I had to figure out how to save money without further jeopardizing city services.

When you're doing something new, you have to expect a bumpy ride. When you're a change agent, you're going to have to knock some heads together. Expectations are high, and people are easily disappointed. I thought of a quote attributed to another Virginian, Woodrow Wilson: "If you want to make enemies, try to change something."

At first, the changes were welcomed. I fired the city manager and brought in a new chief of police who instituted a very effective community policing program. I enlisted community leaders, forming task forces on policy and practice. Everyone was eager to help get the city moving again.

However, entrenchment is a characteristic of bad government, and the roots of dysfunction were deep. I still had to deal with a city council that had grown accustomed to not being challenged. When I tried to hold the members accountable, they sued me and won. It was an unpleasant ordeal, but I was determined to make it clear that I was not beholden to anyone, including the business leaders who had so enthusiastically supported my campaign. I was angry that the business community had allowed a major development project—a concert hall in downtown Richmond—to languish with inadequate funds and poor planning. The city had pledged $27 million, and the center's board had promised to raise the rest of the money, which it hadn't done. There were other issues as well. I was unhappy with the operation of the Greater Richmond Partnership, which had vowed to bring jobs to Richmond, yet I was seeing most of the jobs going to surrounding counties. When I made my unhappiness known, I lost some business support, but I wasn't about to be a rubber stamp for the business community. I would support these efforts only insofar as they helped the city.

But undoubtedly, the most controversial and public tussle occurred with the school board and its administrative offices, which were located on six floors of city hall. In my mind, the school superintendent and the school board were running the show without any regard for the budget. They expected public money but did not accept public accountability. The waste was untenable. And one of the biggest sources of that waste was their tenancy at city hall. I wanted the school board to relocate to a rental building and open up room for the offices of economic development. The city council backed the school board against me and gave it a five-year tenancy contract.

I did not believe the city council had the right to do that, and I ordered the school board to leave, which they refused to do. In an action that many criticized as "imperial" but that I felt was completely within my authority, I ordered the school administration evicted from city hall in a nighttime action involving more than one hundred movers and police oversight. Outraged school board members raced to court to stop the eviction, and a temporary restraining order was issued by a judge. Eventually, the court ruled that I didn't have the authority to evict the school board.

I disagreed with that decision, and I made absolutely no apologies for my actions. I was elected as a change agent with the new power of the office, and there was only one way for progress to happen, and that was for a system of tough accountability and fiscal integrity to take hold. Instead, too often, the old corrupt system forced its way back, like weeds pushing up through the cracks in a sidewalk.

In spite of constant resistance, the four years I was mayor, we got things done. Crime was measurably reduced, infrastructure was repaired, and new businesses were brought to the city. I arranged for "just in time" financing that would put $300 million in the accounts for the construction of fifteen new schools. And I oversaw the first audit of the Richmond public schools, which signaled a vital shift toward accountability.

I declined to run for reelection but felt proud of my four-year term. I had paved the way for a renewal. It was ultimately up to the people of Richmond to decide what they would do with it. However, as I left office in 2008, the nation was facing the worst recession since the Great Depression. This put extra pressure on the city and was a huge setback for already struggling home owners, but today, as the economy recovers, the city is on the right track. The rap on me as mayor was that I was too aggressive, and it was often said that my successor, Dwight Jones, was elected because he had a softer, more mild-mannered image. But Jones, who as a state delegate had opposed the change in charter that allowed for an elected mayor, has discovered that it takes a strong hand to run a city. You have to grab the reins of power with both hands.

⸻

As I was stepping away from the mayor's office in 2009, President Barack Obama was taking the oath of office. It did not surprise me that the American people had chosen an African American as president. I had predicted that inevitability back when I took my own oath of office as governor. However, I was less certain that it would happen in my lifetime.

Then came a young senator named Barack Obama. I was among the first to strongly endorse his nomination. This was more controversial than one might imagine. At the time, the majority of the Congressional Black Caucus and most African American leaders were squarely behind the nomination of Hillary Clinton. The Clintons had deep ties in our community. (Let's not forget that Bill Clinton was so warmly received that he was dubbed the "first black president.") But there were other issues at play. One was a positive—a sense that the African American vote had matured and become more judicious; it did not blindly support a candidate solely based on his race. But there were also conflicts in our community's cautious reception to Obama that were demographic and generational. Obama was a political leader who did not "come up" through the civil rights movement, and he did not speak the common language of struggle and redemption. Many African American leaders who had been battling for decades to achieve a foothold saw him as callow and entitled. They said he hadn't paid proper homage. A clear example of this came the weekend Obama announced his candidacy. That weekend, I was a panelist for a Black Family Summit at Hampton University, hosted by Tavis Smiley. At the same time, Obama was in Springfield, Illinois, announcing he was running for president. I heard a lot of grumbling in the room and some hurt feelings stemming from a year-old grievance. Obama had been invited to the Black Family Summit the previous year but had declined, offering to send his wife, Michelle, to represent him; the offer was refused, and a grudge formed.

But to my surprise, the most contentious discussion involved Obama's choice of an event honoring Abraham Lincoln to make his announcement. One of the panelists was Lerone Bennett, former senior editor at *Ebony* magazine, the premier African American publication. Bennett had just written a book titled *Forced into Glory: Abraham Lincoln's White Dream*, in which he called Lincoln a racist. Now he publicly derided Obama, saying he chose to be in Springfield, Illinois, commemorating a racist and therefore lacked the credentials to carry the torch for African Americans.

I thought that was over the top, and later I asked a good friend, John Hope Franklin, the most renowned African American historian of modern times, what he thought of Bennett's remarks. Franklin said he'd tried to discourage Bennett from writing the book, and he disagreed with his claim that Lincoln was a racist. Parenthetically, Lincoln remains one of my political heroes.

However, Bennett's criticism of Obama certainly fed the mood of the conference. I was disturbed to hear Charles Ogletree, a noted Harvard professor, speak in paternalist terms, describing how both Barack and Michelle Obama were students of his at Harvard Law School and that Barack Obama still had a lot to learn.

And then there was plain old fear. African American leaders were afraid that Obama would get beaten so badly that it would set their cause back a few election cycles. They wanted him to wait until the time was right.

This perspective among our own people endeared me to Obama. I could well recall how many times I had been counseled to wait, how many times I'd been told that people weren't ready. In my mind, Obama was as strong a candidate as I'd seen in a generation. Why wait?

In 2008, the nation felt battered after eight years of war in two countries, a rapidly unraveling economy, and a hardening partisan divide that stymied progress on nearly every front. Obama had first come to public attention with his soaring address at the Democratic convention in 2004, and what impressed people most was the message of healing he brought to the question of race. He became a symbol of what people liked to call a postracial era. While the idea of a postracial era was a fantasy, the point was that Obama, with his wonderful oratory and energy, seemed best able to bring us to a renewal of our shared principles.

For a time after I endorsed Obama, I was a voice in the wilderness. I received a lot of blowback. On one occasion, I went to a Baptist convention in Atlanta to speak for Obama. The presiding official, a prominent pastor from a large northeastern city, relegated me to just being recognized, as he had already committed to Clinton. This was not a solitary incident.

On the ground, though, African Americans were showing up in huge numbers at primaries to vote for Obama. They were impressed that he addressed some of the most sensitive issues of race openly. I think Obama was helped with both African Americans and whites when he gave a soaring speech on race called "A More Perfect Union." In simple, eloquent oratory, he told his story:

I am the son of a black man from Kenya and a white woman from Kansas. I was raised with the help of a white grandfather who survived a depression to serve in Patton's army during World War II and a white grandmother who worked on a bomber assembly line at Fort Leavenworth while he was overseas. I've gone to some of the best schools in America and lived in one of the world's poorest nations. I am married to a black American who carries within her the blood of slaves and slave owners—an inheritance we pass on to our two precious daughters. I have brothers, sisters, nieces, nephews, uncles, and cousins, of every race and every hue, scattered across three continents, and for as long as I live, I will never forget that in no other country on Earth is my story even possible.

And he went on to speak honestly about the grievances that formed on both sides of the racial divide. No presidential candidate had ever been in a position—or been courageous enough—to speak these frank truths. I believe that speech woke up the nation and turned its attention toward Obama. And gradually, the previously reluctant African American leadership began to bend toward his candidacy.

That's not to say that the Democratic Party was fully ready for an African American candidate. After the election, it was revealed that no less a figure than Senate Majority Leader Harry Reid said that Obama had a good chance of winning because he was "light skinned" and had no "Negro dialect." I called on Reid to apologize, and he did, but it goes to show how deep and subversive those harmful stereotypes are.

By the summer, heading into the Democratic national convention in Denver, it appeared that Obama was unbeatable. The only thing standing in the way of his victory was the fate of the superdelegates. I find the term and concept particularly galling, as it not only suggests that some delegates are superior to others but also legally constitutes the same. Superdelegates are members of Congress and the Senate, state officials, and other insiders whose vote is given equal weight to those of the people. They represent 20 percent of the delegates. In the lead-up to the 2008 convention, they were being urged to get behind Clinton and stop an Obama nomination. There was a great deal of tension before Clinton finally rose to speak, pledging her support and her delegates to Obama.

When the Republicans nominated John McCain, along with the virtually unknown Alaska governor Sarah Palin, they cemented Obama's victory. Palin and her cohorts pushed McCain out of his comfort zone— veering rightward when the national mood was more centrist. The Republicans ceded the African American vote to Obama, not even attempting to address that community. Nor did they appeal to the growing Hispanic voter base. Obama won with a coalition of African American, white, Hispanic, and youth votes. The only place he did not get white support was in the Deep South. He won Virginia with 39 percent of the white vote.

"Hope and change" were words shouted from the rooftops on inauguration day in 2009, but I was only cautiously optimistic. I tempered my happiness with a realistic perspective. The crisis in the economy and the lingering wars were enormous boulders in Obama's path that would test his mettle. I couldn't resist contemplating my own history—recalling the glorious moment of my election as the first African American governor. There was a giddy sense that in breaking that barrier, I had lifted African Americans to new opportunities—that doors and windows were flinging open to usher in fresh air. And that was all true, but governing was still a messy business.

The late governor Mario Cuomo famously said, "We campaign in poetry but govern in prose." The real work of governing and living in a society involves generations, not moments, and sometimes it feels as if we take steps back on the way forward. In many ways, Obama's election heightened our awareness of the clash involving demographics and ideology. Entire segments of the population remained incapable of recognizing the equality of African Americans; Latinos; women; the lesbian, gay, bisexual, and transgendered community; and others. And while the people at large called for change, the old voices often sounded louder—just as I experienced the remnants of the Byrd machine still clinging to views long abandoned by the general population.

Partly because of high expectations, partly because of an organized opposition, and partly because of President Obama's own flaws, the true promise of his first term was never realized. Many of his supporters argue that the Republicans in Congress never gave him a chance, that an embedded racism bubbled up from the earth (especially in the South), and that a talented and promising leader was stymied at every turn. I have heard all of those complaints, and I don't entirely disagree. Few presidents have come into office with party control of both houses of Congress and failed to achieve their priorities.

But I still felt from the outset that President Obama was overly cautious in his approach, especially when race was the issue. The disastrous and widely mocked "beer summit" early in his term, when the president tried to serve as a broker between African American scholar Henry Louis Gates and a Boston cop who falsely arrested him, seems to have soured him on taking an active role in racial issues. The unfair firing of Shirley Sherrod from her job as Georgia's director of rural development in 2010, based on a doctored tape by a right-wing blogger, symbolized the administration's skittishness about even the barest hint of preference. Sherrod was falsely accused by the Obama administration of discriminating against white farmers, a false and particularly disturbing charge against a woman who had devoted her life to her community and who didn't have a racist bone in her body—as was plainly demonstrated when the truth came out. The administration didn't even bother investigating the claim before relieving Sherrod of her duties in an abrupt cell phone call. By the time the facts exonerated Sherrod, the damage was done to her reputation and career.

In his history, Obama had been thoughtful and even profound on social issues, and it's the main reason he was elected president. But like so many politicians, he became a tool of his advisers as they tried to sway in cadence with the political winds. Too often, he was a president whose main goal seemed to be not making anyone mad. As a result, he achieved the opposite.

During the president's first term, organizations representing African Americans were particularly sidelined and even directly insulted. President Obama and his administration seemed utterly tone deaf to the voice of the African American community. Two years into his presidency, the president spoke to a gathering of the Congressional Black Caucus about the Republican resistance to his programs. At that event, he told them, "I'm going to press on for the sake of all those families who are struggling right now. I don't have time to feel sorry for myself. I don't have time to complain. I am going to press on. I expect all of you to march with me and press on. Take off your bedroom slippers, put on your marching shoes. Shake it off. Stop complaining, stop grumbling, stop crying. We are going to press on. We've got work to do, CBC." His infuriating paternalism did not sit well with the members. Blaming the failure to get his economic proposals through Congress on black *whining* and chastising the members as if they were bad children was the kind of aloof dismissal that became Obama's signature style. His demeanor, whether intended or not, was not conducive to a positive spirit in the African American community. I didn't believe that African Americans should have expected him to correct all of the mistakes of the past, make race a staple of his presidential concerns, or bear the burden of recognizing and correcting the travails of a race of people with whom he claimed a degree of ethnic relationship. But nor should he have been apologetic. He should not have scolded the petitioners for justice and fair play or publicly lectured the representatives of those legitimate grievances. Had I been in the audience that day, I would have felt insulted.

This was not the "hope and change" president we had expected. This administration too often turned its back on core supporters in favor of holding hands with its enemies under the theory, first advanced by Lyndon Johnson, that it is better to have them inside the tent pissing out than outside the tent pissing in. This was small comfort to African Americans, who had come out in record numbers to vote for Obama and make his victory possible.

I was running into conflicts with the White House. The complaint in the administration was that I wasn't a team player, but I never wanted to play on a team that did not care what I thought or what was important to me. I never learned how to compromise with principle. Yes, I sometimes criticized the president because I never surrendered the right to demand what is right or to criticize what is wrong.

One skirmish came in 2009 when I refused to endorse Creigh Deeds, the Democratic candidate for Virginia governor against Bob McDonnell. The administration burned up the phone lines trying to force an endorsement—including a personal call from the president—but I had a very simple test for endorsements: a candidate's position on the issues. This test transcended party affiliation. Deeds failed the test not only because his positions were too conservative but also because they challenged some of my deepest-held convictions—in particular, the importance of the one-gun-a-month law.

I had some history with Deeds on this matter. When he ran for attorney general in 2005, I refused to support him then because he vowed to repeal the law. Now he was renewing his pledge, and my position on the matter was absolutely clear: "The present law [in Virginia] permits anyone of sufficient age, who is not a felon, to be able to buy one gun a month; twelve a year, twenty-four a year for couples, etc. . . . Mr. Deeds thinks that's not enough and signed a pledge to repeal that law. This action would allow the truckloads of guns to come back in exchange for drugs from those northeastern states where gun laws are more stringent."

When the president called me to urge my support for Deeds, I explained that I had worked hard through the years to get the one-gun-a-month law passed and that Deeds had made a pledge to work to repeal that law.

The president explained what Deeds's election would mean to him in his first foray into state elections since his election to the presidency. Chris Christie was thumping John Corzine in New Jersey, the only other state to hold a gubernatorial election that year. I asked incredulously if the president understood what this meant to me—and, more importantly, what it meant to millions of Virginians who benefited from our commonwealth no longer being considered the gun capital of the United States. Obviously, my demurral was considered a rebuke. McDonnell, who had previously endorsed my law while in the state senate, also said he would repeal it if it hit his desk as governor. That wasn't reason enough for me to change my principled stand against Deeds.

After McDonnell was elected, Deeds became his right-hand man in helping to repeal the one-gun-a-month law, even though the move was opposed by former Republican attorney general Richard Cullen, who had also served as the federal prosecutor for the eastern district of Virginia.

My old colleague Paul Goldman weighed in. In a strong article for *Blue Virginia* titled "McDonnell/Deeds vs. Wilder/Cullen on Guns. Who's Right?," he wrote, "As Justice Holmes said, the law is the only thing keeping human nature from going back into the jungle of social, political and economic Darwinism. It will be interesting to see if former Governor Wilder goes to the 'mat,' as they say, to get Governor McDonnell to show the public law enforcement in Virginia is about stopping the bad guys, not about handcuffing the police." Unfortunately, we did not prevail.

Interestingly, now Senator Kaine, former chairman of the Democratic Party, and President Obama are calling for stricter gun laws. It is refreshing to see the scales fall from their eyes, but it would have been more refreshing to see it before all these national tragedies occurred. They had no problem supporting Deeds, whose vote, along with Edwards's, killed Virginia's one-gun-a-month bill.

Of course, I was accused of being a spoiler, my failure to endorse Deeds tantamount to handing the endorsement to McDonnell. You can see it that way if you're only playing politics. But it's also a corruption of ideals. Party loyalty at all costs is too high a price to pay. Time and again, African Americans are asked to blindly support Democratic candidates, yet when it comes time to collect on the promises, the door is closed.

A glaring example is the U.S. Supreme Court. Most presidents never get the opportunity to appoint members of the Court. President Obama has had two such opportunities. I would have bet the barn and the rent money that given the opportunity, he would have responded wisely. Yet I can't name a single African American who was seriously considered for an appointment to the bench. Were there no sufficiently qualified African Americans to hold such posts and be confirmed by the Senate?

When you consider the present conduct of the Court and its sole African American member, the picture is far from encouraging. During his confirmation hearings, Clarence Thomas repeatedly spoke of his concerns about the rights of the accused and the constitutional protections of criminals. He even told the committee members, "There but for the grace of God go I."

Yet only four months into his term, he proved his insincerity. The case before the Supreme Court involved a man named Keith Hudson, who while in prison was shackled and beaten by two guards who split his lip, loosened his teeth, and broke his dental plate. No less a figure than President George H. W. Bush, who had appointed Thomas to the Court, supported Hudson's claim of cruel and unusual punishment. Justice Sandra Day O'Connor and six other justices concluded that the actions of the prison guards did indeed constitute cruel and unusual punishment, which the Eighth Amendment forbids.

Then Justice Thomas weighed in with a dissent. "The Eighth Amendment is not, and should not be turned into, a National Code of Prison Regulation," he wrote. Thomas's dissent equated Hudson's complaint to gripes about prison food and accused the court majority of stretching the scope of the Bill of Rights. His dissent led the *New York Times* to attack him editorially with a headline reading, "The Youngest Cruelest Justice."

Some of us have longer memories than others, but there are things one should never forget. Justice Thomas, repeatedly and regularly, forgets. That is why I have never understood why President Obama didn't see the need to elevate a second African American to the court—one who had felt the pain of legal segregation, denial, and disparagement.

During that period, I was also disappointed in the state of the Democratic Party in Virginia. Little, if anything, was heard from the Democratic Black Caucus, and that certainly undermined the strength of the party. There was an odd lack of organization in the party as a whole. When I spoke to good Democrats, that is, engaged party members (the backbone of our efforts), they would tell me they'd had no conversations with the leadership and were only rarely consulted. Why would that be the case? It might be suggested that today's incarnation of the Democratic Party of Virginia is built for those who stand as statewide and national candidates at the expense of its rank-and-file members and the ordinary voters of Virginia.

When a gubernatorial primary candidate brought one of his campaign aides to my office during the 2009 election cycle, he noted that the gentleman was a former executive director of the Democratic Party of Virginia. I am an engaged political observer and participant, not to mention a former Democratic elected official. I had never heard that campaign aide's name before or had any occasion to converse with him privately or publicly. I was growing tired of candidates who merely viewed the party obligation as filling out a line on a ballot.

I felt strongly that Virginia Democrats must again engage in an era of grassroots party building to reinvigorate who we are and what we will be. The dispirited mood on the national level seemed to be seeping down to the state, and it was a matter of some concern. What did the Democratic Party stand for? What was its role for the coming decade?

As the 2012 election season got under way, with President Obama's reelection at stake, I did not readily jump in to endorse him as I had done the first time. I felt he should be judged on the fulfillment of promises, and he fell short. It was more than just the tone of his administration. It went deeper.

I was in Washington, D.C., one weekend for a board meeting at Howard University, and though I did not attend any of the Congressional Black Caucus events, I had occasion to talk with people from around the country as well as several members of the caucus, including some senior members. Collectively, they expressed a view that the president needed to toughen up and be less conciliatory. And he needed to focus more attention on the group that had been hardest hit in terms of unemployment, increases in poverty, and overall lack of opportunity.

From the time of the Bush tax cut extensions, the bank bailouts, and the debt ceiling compromise, many Americans, especially African Americans, have wondered aloud, "When is our time coming?" We all had vivid memories of the leadership and vision Obama displayed in his first campaign. Nowhere was the promise of his election more deeply felt than in our community. Yet in the fourth year of the president's term, they were left wondering, "How long?" Practically speaking, this was a problem for Obama's reelection effort. He needed an energized base to win. He could not afford to take the African American electorate for granted.

When I traveled around the state and the country, I was distressed by the deep well of unhappiness I felt as voters repeatedly described the ways in which they were worse off than they'd been at the beginning of

President Obama's term. I kept hearing that although he had run for office as a fiscal moderate, in governing, he leaned too far to the left and was not picking his battles wisely. Jobs, which should have been the centerpiece of his administration, had taken a backseat to other issues. Unemployment was still hovering around 8 percent. The business community was solidly arrayed against him. When it came to the nuts and bolts of governing, his record lacked strength and purpose. Many felt he was disengaged. Too often, he was tone deaf.

Speaking of tone deaf, Vice President Biden didn't exactly help correct that image. Biden had a way of stepping on his tongue, and he drew a cry of outrage when he told an African American audience in Virginia that if Mitt Romney won, his party was going to "put y'all back in chains." I got criticized myself when I said Biden was a tar baby that Obama was stuck with. I made no apologies. Unfortunately, it was true.

A week before the 2012 election, I announced that I would not be endorsing President Obama for reelection. Nor would I endorse Romney. My phone rang off the hook. The indignation level was high. I shrugged it all off. If the president wanted my support in his second term, he had to start earning it.

But the first two years of Obama's second term were a daily battle. As his favorability ratings plummeted and Congress resisted his every move, plenty of pundits were writing his presidential obituary while he had two years remaining in office. His decision to focus on health care rather than jobs did a lot of damage with even his most fervent African American supporters. During the 2013 Virginia gubernatorial campaign, Democrat Terry McAuliffe was leading the Republican lieutenant governor Ken Cuccinelli by double digits until President Obama came to campaign for him and hung the unpopular Obamacare around his neck. Suddenly, McAuliffe's numbers sank, and people started referring to Cuccinelli as "Lazarus." McAuliffe ultimately won, but his margin was less than three points.

But out of the doom and gloom came the president's uncanny ability to upset a negative narrative. As I write this, Obama is entering the final two years of his historic presidency. I found it quite meaningful that in his sixth State of the Union address, on January 20, 2015, having lost Democratic control of Congress in the 2014 election, he returned to his grounding, repeating the oratory that had first brought him to the attention of the nation in 2004: "There is not a liberal America and a conservative America—there is the United States of America. There is not a Black America and a White America and Latino America and Asian America—there's the United States of America." Newly energized, aware that his time to make history was brief, the president seemed refreshed and strong as he began his seventh year in office. Having governed a nation that was increasingly defined by its separations and its gridlock, he was ready to try once more to bring the country together under a common banner—and, failing that, to lead beyond the stalemates of the pack with executive actions.

Being governor of Virginia places one in a rare fraternity. It is impossible to convey the responsibility and rigor of the position to one who has not held it. For this reason, I have cordial, even warm, relationships with most other governors regardless of party. Two of them—George Allen and Jim Gilmore—participated in a 2014 panel discussion at the Virginia Commonwealth University commemorating the twenty-fifth anniversary of my election; and others, including Chuck Robb and Mark Warner, showed up for a celebration. In spite of our differences, we all understood each other pretty well.

I had always had a cordial relationship with Bob McDonnell, who defeated Creigh Deeds and was elected governor in 2009. I had known Governor McDonnell for many years; his children were in strollers when he and his wife, Maureen, first approached me at a speech in Virginia Beach.

Even though he would ultimately end my one-gun-a-month bill as governor, we first bonded over that issue while I was governor. At that time, McDonnell was a big supporter of reasonable measures of gun control, and he didn't mind bucking the Republican Party.

McDonnell understood public service the same way I did. He was passionate about making government more effective, and he was extremely proud to serve in a state that was the cornerstone of the founding of the nation. He considered public life a higher calling. As governor during the recession, he focused like a laser on jobs and the economy and never wavered. I didn't always agree with him, but he was a pretty good governor.

McDonnell and I shared another trait: We loved people and truly enjoyed representing them. We also shared the increasingly lost art of working across the aisle to get things done.

There is no question in my mind that McDonnell would have gone on to seek higher office as a presidential or vice-presidential candidate. He was on everyone's short list. That made his abrupt fall from grace all the more tragic.

In a stunning blow to his personal ambitions, McDonnell and his wife were indicted in early 2014 for receiving gifts and loans in an illegal quid pro quo with a Virginia businessman. The seamy details that emerged during the ensuing trial delighted voracious reporters who happily highlighted the most embarrassing incidents. Overnight, McDonnell went from being a person of dignity and achievement to an object of ridicule.

I saw him occasionally after the indictment, and he looked pale and wasted. The image that came to mind was the Greek myth of Prometheus bound to a stake while an eagle flew in to feast on his constantly rejuvenating liver—a steady torture that did not kill but caused terrible suffering. I was saddened when he was convicted. For me, this was not entertainment; it was disaster.

As a lawyer, I was of two minds about McDonnell's plight. I had no doubt that he was guilty of some wrongdoing, whether deliberately or carelessly. I didn't particularly care for the way his defense tried to make his wife, Maureen, the scapegoat. In many respects, his defense was an embarrassment, his conviction a self-inflicted wound.

On the other hand, I wasn't sure McDonnell's actions rose to a level of criminal and moral turpitude claimed by the prosecution. For this reason,

I agreed to testify as a character witness at McDonnell's sentencing hearing. I advocated for leniency based on McDonnell's past contributions to the state and the good I believed he could still do. I told the court, "Without question, had he not run into the difficulty, he would have been ranked as one of the best governors that Virginia has ever had. And so with those two things [the presidency and vice presidency] now removed from the plate, he has been punished, been punished indelibly, forever. . . . There is no magic wand that can be waved to take away that taint relative to what his reputation was and what it could be and what it might be. And yet, I'm most confident that there are any numbers of persons that see so much good in him that they would like to see that good continue. . . . If Bob McDonnell were to be given fifty years, it wouldn't be any more punishment in terms of how he has suffered. So it is not the measurement of the time; it is what do you do. He has been stigmatized already. He has been hurt and wounded, almost permanently. So I would think it would be, within the court's discretion, of course, to temper justice with mercy."

I also tried to explain some of the realities of the high-pressure daily life as a governor. I spoke of a troubling occurrence in the governor's office, soon after I was elected, when a constituent came to see me, and when I said I was glad to give him a hearing, he replied, "Good. It cost me enough money."

I stared at him, not comprehending. "You paid money to see me?" I asked.

He described the way various people would make offers that they could get people in to see the governor if they'd do one thing or another, including making campaign donations or supporting favored programs. I was hardly a babe in the woods, but this behavior made me extremely unhappy. I let it be known among my staff and supporters that the way constituents could get access to me was to call the receptionist.

In relating this story at McDonnell's sentencing hearing, I was describing a factor that every public official experiences and has to address. Vigilance must be constant. Unfortunately, McDonnell failed to be vigilant.

Yet as I watched him being sentenced to two years in jail, I could not resist making the prediction that we hadn't seen the last of him. Redemption is a favorite theme in American life.

CHAPTER NINE

Reclaiming the Devil's Half Acre

I WAS FIFTY-EIGHT YEARS OLD BEFORE I VISITED A SLAVE HOUSE. I'VE never known my exact roots or where my family was from. I know only that at some point long ago, my ancestors set sail for America from Africa, chained and against their will. Perhaps their first stop was Virginia, or perhaps it was elsewhere. That's a piece of family history I cannot verify. An author researching my background in 1985 asked a state archivist when the first of my family was brought to North America from Africa. No words were minced in response: "They didn't keep track of their property in those days any more than we keep track of people's automobiles today." Actually, we keep better track of automobiles today than they kept of the lives of slaves in antebellum Virginia. But eventually my ancestors arrived there.

Growing up the grandson of slaves, I have always been deeply aware of the inheritance that lives in my blood and bones. It was never abstract for me, but the pilgrimage I made as governor of Virginia to the African nation where so many slaves departed was a life-changing event. I was in Senegal on the first stop of a seven-nation tour, and as I arrived at the University of Dakar to give a speech, I was stopped in my tracks by an enormous banner: "Welcome home, native son Douglas Wilder." I felt a great surge of emotion and understanding when I saw that banner. I was coming to them as a son of Virginia, but, indeed, I was their son too.

When I addressed the faculty at the University of Dakar, they were rapt as they listened to my story. "No one thought a man of color could balance a budget," I told them, and everyone cheered, understanding the impact of that simple truth.

On the island of Goree, off the coast of Senegal, I toured some of the earliest and most despicable slave houses of West Africa. These were the places of no return, where millions of Africans passed on their way to cargo ships. In the compound, I saw how human beings were stuffed into bins, inspected and priced like products, branded like cattle, and packed into the holds of ships. As I stood in the hallway looking out through the famed "Door of No Return," I saw the endless Atlantic Ocean through the despairing eyes of the shackled men and women.

The hopelessness they felt was warranted for their own lives, but they could not have known how heroically they would rise to claim dignity in the face of inhumanity. My sorrow was mixed with pride for the challenges that my ancestors conquered in their new land. Could I have been so courageous as to answer slavery with dignity? My ancestors, in spite of their shackles, raised families, taught values, and helped to build a mighty nation. Their godly contribution is the blood and treasure of our country.

As I toured Africa, I could not help but flash back to my own past. I was reminded of how I was born into a segregated society; how, even after I served my country in Korea on the front lines, I had to leave my own state to attend law school; and how, despite all of the obstacles put in my way, I was able to make a good living, raise three wonderful children, and, with the support of open and fair-minded Virginians, become the nation's first elected African American governor.

Staring out from the "Door of No Return," I marveled that I could return as governor of the state to which my slave forebears had been shipped in bondage. I've never been an overly sentimental man, but the experience rocked me. It was unfathomable that a mere generation separated me from the slave state in Virginia. I was born into the light of an unchained age—but only just barely.

I returned from Africa with a single thought burning in my mind: We had to tell the story and keep our history alive as a charge of eternal vigilance. That's when I came up with the idea of creating the U.S. National Slavery Museum. Although slavery was a worldwide institution, its role in American history has never been fully told. The stories have been too anecdotal and too politically skewed, especially for southerners. The devastating effects of the dehumanization of the Negro in America continue to this day. The American slavery story began with the first shipment of slaves to Jamestown in 1619—although the practice of slavery did not become legal until twenty years later.

How many people are aware that the idea of breeding slaves originated with our most beloved founding father, Thomas Jefferson? That concept was developed to advance the sale of slaves as property, not to have them just for purposes of labor. It released Jefferson from his financial straits, and he advised his son-in-law and other relatives and business associates to follow suit. Slavery was not just a despicable waste of human life; it was a major engine of the economy. Both the American government and the Christian church approved the practice. Twelve U.S. presidents were slave owners, and many of our earliest presidents—including Washington, Jefferson, Madison, Monroe, and Jackson—actually had slaves serving them in the White House. The men who declared that "all men are created equal" did not believe that humanity belonged to the black man.

These are hard and painful truths that many would like to soften with stories of benevolent slave owners—as I so vividly encountered when I challenged the romanticized lyrics of the Virginia state song, "Carry Me Back to Ol' Virginny."

If the history of slavery in America is not taught in the homes, the schools, the pulpits, and the media and if the impact slavery has had on America is not exposed, America will suffer, and our image around the world will be diminished. We will be laying a false claim to being the moral leader of the world. In high school, I learned, "What you do speaks so loudly that I cannot hear what you say." I saw the slavery museum as a way to act loudly.

I have always been impressed by the determination of the Jewish community to ensure that the Holocaust is remembered. I would be surprised to find any Jewish child who does not know about the Holocaust. There are Holocaust museums in every major city in America and a National Holocaust Museum in the nation's capital. I have visited the cemeteries and museums in Poland and Israel. The Jewish story is amazing, and it is still unfolding. The Holocaust didn't even happen in this country. But the message is embedded in the conscience of the world: "Never forget." Observing the remarkable vigilance of the Jewish people only strengthened my determination to do the same for the slave story.

When I returned from my African trip, I began to meet with African American scholars, such as the late John Hope Franklin, and business leaders to discuss the creation of a slavery museum. We created a board and got to work. In the beginning, the board thought that the best location was Jamestown, Virginia, the place where the first Africans were brought. But bogged down in property rights issues and litigation, we had to abandon that plan.

We next approached the city of Richmond about locating the museum there, but the city failed to act. Finally, in 2001, we changed course and settled on a beautiful piece of land in Fredericksburg, overlooking the Rappahannock River—thirty-eight acres donated by the Silver Company at the Celebrate Virginia Retail and Tourism complex. We hoped to open the museum by 2004, but that plan was overly ambitious. It's hard to fully explain why the project got so badly bogged down, but it might have been the location in Fredericksburg—off the beaten track for tourism. In any case, the years passed with difficulty raising money, huge tax bills levied on the property, and countless court battles.

In the midst of our effort, the United States and the entire world was plunged into a historically deep recession. The United States National Slavery Museum was not immune from the blight. Fund-raising for the museum became more challenging. Some critics thought we were in competition with fund-raising efforts for the Underground Museum in Cincinnati and/or the African American museum then being contemplated in the nation's capital. I was unaware that one of our board members was also a board member of the Underground Museum. We floundered. By 2012, the city of Fredericksburg, which had elected not to grant the museum tax-exempt status as the federal government had done, attempted to sell the property at public auction for unpaid taxes. With the help of many people, that was avoided. Still, people began to doubt that the museum would ever come to be.

I never gave up hope. By 2012, my gaze had traveled back to my home in Richmond, where the museum should have been all along.

———

My father was not one to talk about slavery and what his parents had been through. Yet when I was a child, we would go to the horse stables in Shockoe Bottom. It is estimated that between 1800 and 1865, an estimated 300,000 to 350,000 slaves were processed through the Shockoe Bottom slave auction blocks in Richmond on their way to the Deep South. My father would point to the site of Lumpkin's Jail. Robert Lumpkin was considered one of the most brutal of slave traders, and his jail, where slaves waited to be sold, was known as "the Devil's half acre." Lumpkin also fathered five children with a former slave called Mary, who took his name and inherited his property. When Lumpkin died, Mary donated the site for an educational institution for freedmen that would evolve into the school we today know as Virginia Union University. So a catalyst for black education, Virginia Union University, was founded in 1865 on a piece of land that formerly was one of the world's most notorious parcels of black hell on earth. After that, the land went from being known as "the Devil's half acre" to "God's half acre."

Lumpkin's Jail represented pure evil turned to hope, and I thought it was the right home for our museum. Our proposed location was also where Richmond's first African American Baptist church was founded.

We immediately began efforts to purchase the property. Governor McDonnell committed $11 million in state funds toward the effort. The Richmond City Council committed an additional $5 million, with the remaining $15 million or so to be raised in private funds and loans. After he was elected governor in 2013, Terry McAuliffe also gave his support for the project. Since that time, I have initiated discussions with Virginia Commonwealth University, present owners of the church site, which had already been deemed a state historical location, for the museum to be located there. Today, we are optimistic that the slavery museum will be ready by 2019 to mark the four-hundredth anniversary of the first slaves arriving in Jamestown.

The facility and institution that history compels us to create will ensure that no one ever forgets the ignominy initiated on these shores—one that tore families apart, scarred portions of this great country's effort to herald freedom and equality, and led to the bloodiest war in American history. This important piece of Virginia presents the American paradox of darkness and light in a manner that cannot be matched.

Enthusiasm in the community runs high. We can more than just imagine a museum, its shelves lined with artifacts and its lobby full of waiting visitors. Many people have donated priceless artifacts of slavery, including dozens of precious documents, which were lovingly put in storage, although some of them are on display at Virginia Union University. The museum will be dedicated to the human rights of all individuals worldwide, some presently enslaved, as slavery has never been a respecter of race, religion, ethnicity, or nationality.

If any further evidence were needed that our slavery museum is an essential piece of history—indeed, an urgent matter—we need only look at the recent rise in slavery denial. Like Holocaust deniers, these slavery "truthers" aim to rewrite the history of slavery in a less damning way. Unable to bear the weight of a shameful chapter in America's past, slavery deniers are recasting it as something more uplifting and consistent with our nation's founding spirit. These chilling efforts ignore the torment and paint a more benevolent picture. I myself have spoken to many people who have made the argument that slaves brought in chains from Africa were ultimately blessed because America was a much better place to be. I have heard people say that many slave owners were like surrogate parents, devoted and loving toward their slaves.

It would be one thing if these attitudes were merely espoused by the ignorant few. However, there have been efforts to codify them into our institutions of learning. In 2010, the Texas State Board of Education attempted to rewrite textbooks referring to slavery as the "Atlantic triangular trade"—whatever that meant—completely eliminating the word *slavery* from the text. A similar effort by the Tennessee Board of Education likewise whitewashed slavery and also eliminated any mention of the violence of the Ku Klux Klan toward African Americans. In both cases, the school boards tried to elevate the founding fathers at the expense of the truth. Representative Michele Bachmann, approving of their efforts, stated in a speech that the founding fathers "worked tirelessly" to abolish slavery—shamelessly ignoring the fact that most of them were slave owners and that the Emancipation Proclamation was issued in 1863, almost a century after the founding of our nation.

More recently, the myth was resurrected that slaves fought enthusiastically in the Confederate army and believed in the cause of the Confederacy. Absent any evidence that such a thing occurred, the "scholars" who promote this fiction are loud and insistent, although their assertions are totally lacking in context. To be sure, there were those slaves who fought in exchange for a promise of freedom, but this hardly amounted to a belief in Confederate principles.

When I hear these dangerous ideas being parlayed and even seeping into textbooks, it strengthens my resolve to get the slavery museum up and running at last. This is an American story worth telling.

America—and especially Virginia—is a land of great contradiction. We believe in our hearts that all men and women are created equal, endowed by our Creator with inalienable rights. And yet we know that this land was soiled with the greatest sin against freedom imaginable. This is the setting of the great American Dissonance, where both the loftiest and the basest ideas coexisted and could not be reconciled. The process of reconciliation, which began when people like my grandparents settled into lives of freedom, is still ongoing. Freedom, dignity, equality, and service are the linchpins of the life I have sought to live in their stead.

I believe that we cannot fully express the American Dream without acknowledging our past. We can express shame and regret without diminishing our nation's promise. We can acknowledge that slavery was hell—that our national policy was to deny African Americans their God-given right to be full selves in freedom. And we can exult in the possibility that in knowing our history, we can determine never to repeat it.

Yet it is impossible to learn from a past of which most of us are ignorant. We see occurrences on a daily basis that remind too many of us that vestiges of the past still influence our present-day activities. Who among us can deny it?

My effort to create a place where the *true* American story of slavery can be told has now lasted more than twenty years. My struggle has constantly been referred to as a "personal crusade," implying that it is something that I would benefit from in some way. Combatting that assumption is one reason I have persisted. This is not a personal crusade but a national necessity.

CHAPTER TEN

Ringing the Bell

SINCE 1989, PEOPLE HAVE ASKED ME CONSTANTLY, "HAVE AFRICAN Americans in America *arrived*?" Two have been elected governors of states. The U.S. Senate has counted African American men and women as part of its membership. African Americans sit in the leadership of the U.S. House of Representatives for both parties. And the people elected an African American to serve as president of the United States. Is that what it means to arrive?

In the early days after the abolition of slavery, an idea gained momentum that the advancement of our race relied on the "talented tenth." That is, if one in ten African Americans were educated and cultivated for leadership, their efforts could lift the rest. Although W. E. B. Du Bois is often credited with this theory, he was in fact not the originator, though he embraced and endorsed it. In his essay "The Talented Tenth," he wrote of the need to grab hold of this intellectual and racial challenge:

> *Men of America, the problem is plain before you. Here is a race transplanted through the criminal foolishness of your fathers. Whether you like it or not the millions are here, and here they will remain. If you do not lift them up, they will pull you down. Education and work are the levers to uplift a people. Work alone will not do it unless inspired by*

the right ideals and guided by intelligence. Education must not simply
teach work—it must teach Life. The Talented Tenth of the Negro race
must be made leaders of thought and missionaries of culture among
their people. No others can do this and Negro colleges must train men
for it. The Negro race, like all other races, is going to be saved by its
exceptional men.

In our modern era, we can easily criticize the "talented tenth" theory as being elitist and in its own way racist in that it presupposes that 90 percent of our population is incapable of higher pursuits. However, the question of leadership remains an urgent matter for the African American community. Where are the exceptional leaders for our day? Why does the silence sound so deafening?

After my term as governor of Virginia, the writer Judson L. Jeffries wrote of the symbolic importance of black leadership: "Symbolic representation is not only desirable but also necessary for African Americans. Black politicians are role models for the black community. Young African Americans, in particular, need to see the Wilders, who look like them, in positions of authority and expertise." And that is certainly true. Yet even as we speak with pride about our African American president, our numbers in the corridors of power are minuscule. I was proud to be the first elected African American governor twenty-five years ago, but since that time, there has been only one other elected (Deval Patrick of Massachusetts) along with one elevated (David Patterson of New York). In the entire history of our nation, there have been only nine African Americans in the U.S. Senate—seven in my lifetime. Only forty-three of 535 members of the House of Representatives are African American—forty Democrats and three Republicans. The giants of African American leadership have included mayors of major cities, such as Tom Bradley, Carl Stokes, Harold Washington, Maynard Jackson, and Richard Hatcher. Yet when one considers the numbers of African Americans elected to real positions of power and influence in America, it should become obvious that it is not enough to rely on elected African Americans to lift our communities.

In the time of abolition and again during the civil rights era, our leadership obviously did not come from the ranks of the elected, as they were essentially nonexistent. But rise up they did. Frederick Douglass, Booker T. Washington, Paul Laurence Dunbar, and others were all educated men. Although some were self-educated, they used their knowledge for the betterment of their people and the nation as a whole.

Without the brainpower supplied by Thurgood Marshall, Spottswood Robinson, Charles Hamilton Houston, and dedicated and selfless lawyers, we might not have achieved core legal successes that paved the way for civil rights: one-person/one-vote (*Baker v. Carr*), the Civil Rights Act, the Voting Rights Act, and Affirmative Action.

Thurgood Marshall's appointment to the Supreme Court was not just the seating of a member who happened to be African American. It was instrumental in educating and informing the fellow justices of the elements of racism: its effects and threats to fulfillment of our commitment to "a more perfect union."

I had occasion to be with Marshall's widow, Cecilia (Cissy), in 2014 at an event commemorating the sixtieth anniversary of *Brown v. Board of Education*. I spoke to her about conditions in America today relative to race and asked her what she thought Thurgood would have to say about it. She smiled, remarking that I knew him well enough to know that his language might haven't sat too well with a public audience.

Every advance is welcome, but I believe that the progress of a community of people must be judged by more than whether individual men and women hold single seats in boardrooms in New York City or even occupy an oval room in Washington, D.C. To limit our definition of progress to singular accomplishments is too easy and too lazy and leaves too many people behind. Even as an African American sits in the White House, our community at large is suffering more than ever from the crushing weight of economic distress. As I write this, the nation's unemployment rate is declining, yet African American unemployment is in the double digits. That is not anyone's definition of arriving. So we must think harder about this, and that includes the need to acknowledge, understand, and respect our history.

There are many committed hardworking people who are fighting the modern battles. But I dare say that if we were asked to name the individuals or groups that are walking in the footprints of their brave and prestigious predecessors, we would be hard-pressed.

As slavery ended 152 years ago, the Emancipation Proclamation served as the ringing of a big bell that announced to enslaved Americans that they were finally to be given what should be a natural right for all men and women: freedom. But as our people were to see over the next few decades, despite President Lincoln's proclamation being enshrined in the Constitution, it was not yet a full American freedom that had been bestowed in practical fact to match the beautiful words.

What was needed was the ringing of a second bell. That happened in 1954 with *Brown v. Board of Education* and continued through the 1960s with the Civil Rights Act and the Voting Rights Act. Has the bell been rung since then? Certainly it has. Many people viewed Barack Obama's election as such a moment. The question is, how do we keep that bell ringing, and whose arms will be lifted to pull those heavy ropes?

We prize this nation's mores and values that push us continually to live up to the ideal of freedom—sometimes despite ourselves—but they do not come to us automatically just because we're Americans. We must work toward them every day; otherwise, they will wither. No isolated event, no single election or bill passed, can cement freedom and equality on its own.

This truly is a continuing project in national community building that none of us has any right to cease. The question of the next few decades is how to march forward during this ongoing struggle. And struggle we will, and struggle we must to keep realizing our rights as inalienable and more universal. Sometimes it can feel as if we are falling down at the job. At the state and local levels, we see anachronistic patterns of thought and downright unimaginable and unfair policies that lead us away from meaningful solutions. We regularly see the results of federal, state, and local policies that are nothing short of disastrous: decreased interest in voting, decreased ability to vote, increased poverty, decreased home ownership, increased homelessness, increased health care costs, decreased ability to seek the protection of bankruptcy for a fresh start, unfair court sentencing, untreated illnesses, and substandard housing. All strengthen the belief by some that collective action through government is not only ineffective but also harmful. I don't share that belief, but we must be vigilant and do better.

We, as a people, are in the process of making monumental decisions about what this country will look like in the future. If I were to give you my progressive checklist, it would begin with asking and answering the following questions:

- How will changes in Social Security, Medicare, Medicaid, national health care, immigration, mental health care, firearms policy, and education impact the poor and people of color?

- What is the responsibility of government to determine, prevent, and reduce the adverse impact of its social policies?

- Will we balance budgets by turning our hearts away from those in the most need? Will we be indifferent to how the policies that are instituted will affect those still fighting to participate more fully in the American Dream? And if we do, is that an America still striving to demonstrate that all men are created equal?

When we look to Washington, it's hard not to yearn for a different era of leadership. But even more than that, this nation needs a better understanding of what policies are necessary for all Americans to live on an equal plane of opportunity and to have an equal stake in the country.

As we decide what those policies will be for the future, we must have governmental actors who understand that. We must have governmental leaders who remember that this nation's instruments of democracy promise fairness and equality to all citizens, not just the ones who can pay the most talented lawyer-lobbyists money can buy.

I found a shocking statistic: Former slaves freed by President Lincoln's Emancipation Proclamation on January 1, 1863, could read and write at a higher rate fifteen years after the end of the Civil War than their descendants can today. That is a damning and downright unacceptable fact. We cannot sustain a nation that strives to stand for justice and opportunity for all if that remains true. We can't generate economic power for all if that remains true. Equality cannot be secure if that remains true. We can do better than that, and we must. Doing so is properly living up to our responsibility to protect the idea that is America.

In 1990, in my first year as governor, I received a call from Terry Sanford, the Democratic senator, former governor of North Carolina, and former president of Duke University. He told me that he wanted to do a study of the plight of the African American male and asked me if I'd cochair. I was instantly on board, and Sanford and I went on to raise funds, hire staff, and gather input from mayors, community leaders, academics, and public figures across the country, including stars from the entertainment industry. Our efforts culminated in the creation of the 21st Century Commission on African American Males. A report was issued, and we held a conference in 1991. We were able to present our data at a Senate hearing that coincided with our gathering. In stunning testimony, former army secretary Clifford L. Alexander Jr., the first African American to hold that position, challenged members of the Senate for being essentially a segregated group. (No African Americans were serving at that time.) He called them "the most segregated body in America." Looking the senators straight in the eye, Alexander spoke a jarring truth: "You see us as less than you are. You think we are not as smart, not as energetic, not as well suited to supervise you as you are to supervise us, that we are looking for something extra—a government program that gives us something we do not deserve." He went on to say, "White men and women can develop the solutions . . . black men can only nibble at the edges of power in America."

It was a dramatic opening for our conference, which was a serious in-depth examination of the daunting social challenges facing African American men in our society. There were many—rising unemployment, disproportionate criminal activity and imprisonment, high illiteracy, and the nation's highest mortality and shortest life expectancy rates. We argued that these problems not only hurt the African American urban community but also extended into the white suburbs and hurt everyone.

The 21st Century Commission on African American Males was an important effort, and we earned a lot of publicity. That's when people started coming out of the woodwork, complaining that their names had not been attached to our efforts. Unfortunately, there are still those who believe that media sound bites are the measurements of progress, and I got many calls asking why certain people and groups were not included. The backlash we ran into from our own community put a slight damper on our efforts. I got a call from Terry, who said that people were expressing to his staff and others that they couldn't understand why he, a white man, was a cochair—much less that it was his idea to start with. They accused him of using the commission as a political stunt to appeal to African American voters in his upcoming election. His pride was such that he said to me, "Doug, I don't need this; I will no longer cochair the effort, but I will support you." I said to him that I would not turn over the group to another, less qualified cochair. So, as often happens when people are trying to do good work, there were some segments of the community that were more concerned with getting credit and having a platform. Leadership is a matter not of big personalities but of big ideas. Until we become more concerned with substance and results than with who gets credit, we're in trouble.

Twenty-two years after our commission, there remains a socioeconomic and racial divide that reflects itself in our social policies and governmental practices. Can you imagine how much more advanced we would have been had we not been infected by the "crabs in the bucket" mentality, which says that "if I can't have it, neither can you"? How we address the divide is the true American question. Sometimes we do it through government. As James Madison said, "If men were angels, no government would be necessary." Government is a call to our better selves. But it also takes the will of the people to be more than their worst impulses. I've never accepted the idea that African Americans are victims. We are responsible for ourselves. And there is a dysfunction in the African American community that we must acknowledge. It's deep-rooted but is often painfully visible in a kind of sloppy cultural behavior that did not exist in prior generations. People might call me old-fashioned, but in their private hearts, they know I am speaking the truth.

When I was coming up, our house was always open for anybody to come and visit. The living room was set apart for guests; we weren't allowed to fool around in there. The same was true for the dining room. There was a china closet with the appropriate china. There was a linen cupboard and a stretching board to make sure all the linens were pristine and without creases. There was a drawer of polished cutlery. My mother was rigorous in assuring that everything be proper, that guests to our home be treated with respect. The message to us kids was clear: You don't need money to have dignity.

In my neighborhood, where people were struggling to get by, the yards were neat and well tended. At our house, we understood that when we got up in the morning, we swept the porch and the sidewalk in front of our house. At least once a year, we whitewashed the fence. Everything was impeccable, and we wouldn't dare question the need for it. Although we lived in a segregated neighborhood and one that was financially lacking, there was a sense of pride that permeated our community and others like it. That sense of house pride is gone in many African American communities. Why does it matter? Think about it. In all of our lives, there are hundreds of ways we get up every day and present ourselves to the world. How we appear and how we behave reflects our respect for ourselves and the human community. It's not superficial. My parents' generation was fighting to gain even the smallest measure of dignity. They understood that no one *gives* you dignity. You cultivate it from the inside.

In the community of my childhood, leadership developed internally through Masonic lodges and churches. Preachers then were part of the fabric. They ate in our homes and walked our streets. They did not rule from the pulpit but gained their influence from everyday actions. Like everyone else who maintained a household, most of them worked jobs just as their congregations did. As the civil rights movement grew, it is notable that the leadership included black ministers, such as Martin Luther King Jr. and others, who expressed their deepest religious principles in the cause of freedom. King used to say, "I am many things to many people. But in the quiet recesses of my heart, I am fundamentally a clergyman, a Baptist preacher." These black clergy sought to wrest religious principle away from the segregationist Christian pulpits and restore it to the people. Remember, in the 1800s, African American churches by law had to be led by white ministers.

I recall as a young boy going to church, which was mandatory in the Wilder household, listening to the calming music and studying the pictures displayed on the stained-glass windows. All the figures were white. There were no angels of color, no children of color sitting at the feet of Jesus, no disciples of color. Jesus and his mother, painted by medieval Europeans, were Caucasian as well. At the time, it seemed just the way it was; I didn't question it. But I've later reflected on how insidiously the portrayal seeped into the consciousness of African American children, making them feel rejected and unholy. The civil rights movement sought, among other things, to enlighten African Americans about their place in God's glory.

Martin Luther King Jr. was not just a minister; he was a theologian, a philosopher, and a teacher. When he preached, his words had the clear purpose of inspiring and uplifting, and he chose them carefully, eloquently linking religious tradition to the practical imperatives on the ground.

The tide of history opened an opportunity for King, and he chose to speak in the language of faith that gave comfort and motivation to his constituency. His most poignant speech was a call to faith delivered at the Mason Temple in Memphis, Tennessee, the day before he was assassinated: "I just want to do God's will," he said, "and he's allowed me to go to the mountain. And I've looked over, and I've seen the Promised Land. I may not get there with you, but I want you to know tonight that we as a people will get to the Promised Land."

The fact that King was a man of the cloth might have led some to believe that his cause was ordained by God—and perhaps it was. Ironically, the African American church was not unified behind the civil rights movement. Some considered King too radical. Dexter Avenue Baptist Church in Montgomery, Alabama, was so opposed to religious activism that it mounted an effort to get rid of the great civil rights leader and King's predecessor, Dr. Vernon Johns. From the pulpit, Dr. Johns advocated demonstrations and boycotts. He was fierce and single-minded, with no time for the gentility of the South.

Sadly, in recent times, the African American community has lost touch with the power of the preacher in enabling civil rights. While the fundamentalist white churches, with the hearts of their congregations hardened against equality, have thrived, too many African Americans are of the mind that religion and politics don't mix. The African American is no longer grounded in the religious teaching that enabled civil rights, and while there are many up-front, principled African American religious leaders, there seems to be a perception that their leadership is not about the betterment of the community but simply about their own betterment. We have to do better.

It's not that I'm calling for more candidates for public office to come from the ranks of church pastors or ministers. I'm asking whether the churches in the African American communities have a new role to play in our progress. I think they do, and I'd welcome their voice.

In the meantime, the infection of poverty and racism spreads in our communities, and this, too, showcases an absence of leadership. When I heard about the events in Ferguson, Missouri, what struck me most was that all the decision makers were white. If the overwhelming majority of a community is African American and the entirety of the leadership is white, that fact should have been addressed long before Michael Brown was killed. The leadership of the groups that then spoke out and demonstrated could not honestly lay claim to concerns on the ground; they didn't live there or work there. There were too many opportunistic spokespersons who diminished the legitimacy of those working tirelessly behind the scenes to lead by correcting the community's wrongs. Opportunistic leaders are not leaders at all. Positioned leadership is one thing; *real* leadership is another. One might have the position, but one must also have the authority that comes from trust. If you have the trust of the people, you can do a lot.

In 1963, when blacks were shut off from opportunity and equality, we responded with the March on Washington. But our memories of that day are clouded; we commemorate the march without recalling its significance or its official title: the March on Washington for *Jobs and Freedom*. It had a purpose well beyond the gathering, as a motivator of policy and performance.

Likewise, while demonstrations may be well and good, during the period of mourning following Brown's death, it would have been more inspiring and more meaningful to flood the area with voting registrars because in America, our power is exercised at the polls. I've been saying this for forty years: We must learn to move into position to bring about change. You can't change things by praying, wishing, hoping, or yelling. You've got to vote and take the power. If you think you're not being represented, the greatest punishment you can inflict upon a politician is to take his or her job away.

We must fight inertia. Today, the American public is not happy with either political party and is disenchanted with politicians in general. People are cynical about Washington gridlock and the petty squabbles that swarm across every issue. They've given up on these pompous purveyors of political speak. I say the time is right for ordinary people to take on the yoke of leadership.

I'm left to wonder how we've gone from a generation that in the depths of segregation was taught that we could achieve the American dream to today, when so much emphasis is on self-interest, violence, and mediocrity. Certainly, there can be no doubt that a historic damage has been done to a great number of people in this country, and there will never be a shortage of people to tell our young that they have no chance in society. I challenge young people to move beyond saying they can't succeed because some entity is holding them back or because government is still in the way or the judicial system and state legislatures are still blocking the path.

Every chance I get, I speak to groups of young people about taking the reins. I've found that, contrary to the regular complaint, young people are incredibly emboldened and attracted to government. The most effective movements of our time are organized by millennials. They're not going to sit on the sidelines and be told what they can't say or do.

I have been gratified to have a school created in my name at Virginia Commonwealth University—the L. Douglas Wilder School of Government and Public Affairs. I teach classes there and am invigorated by the challenge of helping to shape young leaders. I am certain that I will see many of them on the public stage. In their midst, I am heartened to find the youth of today every bit as probing, questioning, and passionate as I was some sixty years ago.

In 2013, I was honored to give the commencement address at the Ailes Apprentice Program, an impressive effort sponsored by Roger Ailes, the chairman of Fox News. I told the group of exceptional young people something they already knew—that they are usually characterized by their elders as entitled, brazen, and hurried. I saw them another way. The words I used to define their generation were *bold, searching, communitarian*, and *tolerant*. "Those are the characteristics that could allow your generation to take command of this nation and to keep it great," I told them. "They will allow you all to continue the American tradition of heralding new scientific accomplishments, continuing the march to greater equality, and serving as a beacon to the less fortunate."

They were responsive to my comments. But it's also clear that in order to make change happen, we have to be smart about it and organized. We have to get our ducks in a row. Unfortunately, what I have witnessed around the country is the absence of the kind of organizations of old that pulled people together and in the process achieved measurable gains for minorities.

These days, it's more common to have spokespeople, mostly self-appointed, delivering puffed-up jeremiads to advance their own cults of personality. If this trend continues, many of the gains made on behalf of the people who have been locked out of the decision-making process will continue to erode. No doubt, there are those who look at the election of Barack Obama as the "magic moment." They will say to those of us who see the need for eternal vigilance, "You had your chance." But our chance has just begun.

That vigilance must root out the underlying racist ideas that often go unnoted. In the 2014 election, some voters in South Carolina were asked whether they agreed or disagreed with a series of statements that, frankly, shock the conscience. Among them were these:

- Blacks are getting too demanding in their push for equal rights.

- It's really a matter of some people not trying hard enough; if blacks would only try harder, they could be as well off as whites.

To even ask these questions indicates a level of ignorance that should have long ago been banished. We have not come so far that we cannot slip back, thus the need for eternal vigilance.

So, have we "arrived"? I would answer that we are still *arriving*.

At a recent social event, I met a young African American man who had just graduated from college. He told me he was interested in running for political office someday and asked my advice. I often get such requests. People are always coming by, saying they want to run for the school board or the city council or the state legislature. When I ask them why, I hear vague answers about their love of children—who the hell doesn't love children?—or their interest in serving. But they lack substance or thought. Many of them view the process of being elected as similar to winning a popularity contest. So when this young man approached me, I asked him if he was serious because the process requires deep thought and selfless action. He nodded that he was serious. So I told him what I've told so many others throughout the years:

"First, don't run for elected office if you can't afford it. If you are married and/or have a family, consider the financial aspects. Second, consider what it is that you offer that is different from those who presently hold that office. Third, and most importantly, don't forget that you are elected to represent the people. Your dedication to those whom you represent is more important than party or financial contributors."

In my lifetime, I've known many individuals who met these criteria. Some of them sought office; others labored in the field. Whenever I can, I impress upon young people the need for them to step forward and join that sacred collective of people who care. It's the right thing to do.

Not long ago, I had occasion to sit down for a conversation with the thoughtful African American NPR journalist Michel Martin. She asked me a profound question: "If you were advising a young Doug Wilder who was just starting out, what words of wisdom would you like to pass on?"

I repeated my mother's words, borrowed from Socrates, which I have carried with me my entire life: "Know you're right, then proceed."

But I added that before you *know* you're right, you've got to get your act together. You've got to study and learn. You've got to ask questions. You've got to do the hard work. I told Michel that when my mother advised me, she couldn't have fully appreciated what she was setting in motion. What she created was an independent thinking man. That's who I am, and that's who every young American is capable of becoming.

ENDNOTES

Chapter One: Carry Me Back

1 *Carry Me Back*: The word "Virginny" had been replaced by "Virginia" in the official version, but it was—and still is—common to hear "Virginny."

3 *On the editorial page*: Editorial, "Some History about a Song," *Richmond News Leader*, February 12, 1970. In addition, a *News Leader* column by Charles Houston (February 10, 1970) took the discussion to another level. Houston quoted Dr. Douglas Southall Freeman's foreword in *A Treasury of Southern Folklore* (New York: Crown, 1949), in which he wrote, "If the Negroes wished to avenge themselves for their bondage, they should say they have made their masters their captives in music, in mimicry, in humor and in laughter. . . . The Negro is the heart of the wisdom and wit of the South."

5 *The letters poured in*: Most of the correspondence referred to the "Negro." Although the term had gone out of general public use in the late 1960s, it was still widely heard in the South, especially by the older generation.

8 *Over the years*: In 2014, Virginia state senator Walter Allen Stosch introduced a bill proposing that "Sweet Virginia Breeze," a song by Robbin Thompson and Steve Bassett, be named the state song.

14 *Patrick Henry gave*: Henry was opposed to slavery and once said, "I believe the time will come when an opportunity will be afforded to abolish this lamentable evil. Everything we can do, is to improve it, if it happens in our day. If not, let us transmit to our descendants, together with our slaves, a pity for their unhappy lot and an abhorrence of slavery."

21 *We attended the*: As Lois Leveen vividly describes in her *New York Times* article "The North of the South" (January 24, 2011), the First African Baptist Church had a storied history in Richmond's slow journey from slavery to emancipation. Initially, the First Baptist Church included both blacks and whites in its membership. When the white membership left to create a separate church in 1841, the First African Baptist Church was formed. Ironically, the white minister appointed to lead its congregation was a slave owner.

22 *In Ransome's*: Carter G. Woodson, *The Story of the Negro Retold* (Washington, DC: Associated Publishers, 1935).

23 *One was a man*: In 1973, the navy commissioned a frigate, the USS *Miller*, in Miller's honor. His story was featured in the 2001 movie *Pearl Harbor*. He was played by the actor Cuba Gooding.

Chapter Two: Sergeant Wilder

28 *I'd read Ralph Ellison's*: Ralph Ellison, *Invisible Man* (New York: Random House, 1952).

30 *President Truman had integrated*: It was not an overnight decision. The effort leading up to Truman's executive order desegregating the military had been under way since the end of World War II. In 1945, Truman's secretary of war appointed a board to investigate the army's policies toward African Americans. Much of the brass recognized that they were an underutilized resource. When the report was issued in 1946, it stated that the military should "eliminate, at the earliest practicable moment, any special consideration based on race." Later that year, Truman appointed the President's Committee on Civil Rights, which issued a stunning report titled *To Secure These Rights*. It was a strong condemnation of segregation in the armed forces and called "to end immediately all discrimination and segregation based on race, color, creed or national origin in . . . all branches of the Armed Services." By 1948, Truman had made the decision to end segregation in the armed forces and the civil service through administrative action (executive order) rather than through legislation, perhaps (rightly) fearing the

blowback from southern Democrats. Indeed, politics was very much on everyone's mind in 1948, a presidential election year. In a riveting speech before the Democratic convention, Minneapolis mayor Hubert H. Humphrey became the first mainstream politician to decisively call for the elimination of segregation in the military—not a position favored by his party, whose platform committee rejected the idea. However, immediately after the convention, on July 26, Truman issued his executive order desegregating the military. He barely won reelection, as the divisions in the party around race began to make themselves felt.

37 *To my amazement*: Dwayne Yancey, *When Hell Froze Over: The Untold Story of Doug Wilder: A Black Politician's Rise to Power in the South* (Dallas: Taylor Publishing, 1988). Yancey was a staff writer for the *Roanoke Times and World-News* who followed my campaign on the ground.

Chapter Three: The Home Trenches

40 *In Virginia, where*: J. Harvie Wilkinson III, *Harry Byrd and the Changing Face of Virginia Politics 1945–1966* (Charlottesville: University of Virginia Press, 1968).

41 *Perhaps unsurprisingly*: The claim in the legislature was for interposition. Interposition asserts the right of an individual state to oppose actions of the federal government that it believes are unconstitutional. Although rarely upheld in court, these assertions continue to this day. Historically, most interposition efforts have involved integration, but most recently the Affordable Care Act (Obamacare) has been the reason for interposition declarations.

43 *In Boynton v. Virginia*: The Supreme Court ruled in *Boynton v. Virginia* on December 5, 1960, that interstate passengers were protected by the Interstate Commerce Act. The seven-to-two ruling, written by Justice Hugo L. Black, turned on the status of the contractor operating the dining area: "We are not holding that every time a bus stops at a wholly independent roadside restaurant the act applies . . . [but] where circumstances show that the terminal and restaurant operate as an

integral part of the bus carrier's transportation service . . . an interstate passenger need not inquire into documents of title or contractual agreements in order to determine whether he has a right to be served without discrimination." It would take many years for African Americans to receive full service without challenge. Indeed, among the most compelling scenes from the civil rights era involve their trying unsuccessfully to be seated at lunch counters in bus stations.

51 *I knew I had*: The impact of Voters Voice is discussed in Lewis A. Randolph and Gayle T. Tate, *Rights for a Season: The Politics of Race, Class, and Gender in Richmond, Virginia* (Knoxville: University of Tennessee Press, 2003).

53 *I was running*: Ralph Eisenberg, "1969 Politics in Virginia: The General Election," University of Virginia Institute of Government, May 15, 1970.

58 *In my remarks*: "All-White Church Rejects Football Star's Family," *Free Lance-Star*, July 9, 1977.

65 *To no one's surprise*: Ben A. Franklin, "Race Erupts in Virginia Governor's Race," *New York Times*, November 2, 1981.

Chapter Four: Political Muscle

71 *My announcement*: Michael Isikoff, "Ex-Firebrand Still Singes Democratic Party," *Washington Post*, May 1, 1982.

71 *On May 4*: Tyler Whitley, "No Independent Race, Wilder Says," *Richmond News Leader*, May 5, 1982.

71 *I had demonstrated*: Dale Eisman, "Wilder Flexed New Political Muscle," *Richmond Times-Dispatch*, May 9, 1982.

72 *The Democrats nominated*: Patricia E. Baner, "Pickett Decision Assures Wide-Open Convention," *Washington Post*, May 5, 1982.

73 *I will say*: Fred Barnes, "Virginia State Senator Wilder Exercises Black Power," *The Sun*, July 11, 1982; Tyler Whitley, "Wilder's Influence Growing—State Senator Emerging as Power Broker," *Richmond News Leader*, July 7, 1982.

Chapter Five: Re-Digging the Well

75 *It wasn't easily*: Dwayne Yancey, *When Hell Froze Over: The Untold Story of Doug Wilder: A Black Politician's Rise to Power in the South* (Dallas: Taylor Publishing, 1988).

76 *Fearing a loss*: Tom Sherwood, "Wilder Bid Worries Some Virginia Democrats: Impact of Black Candidates on Other Races Weighed," *Washington Post*, November 15, 1984.

76 *In December*: Larry Sabato was the voice everyone was listening to when it came to Virginia politics—and he still is. From his home at the University of Virginia, he publishes *Sabato's Crystal Ball*, which gives valuable analysis and predictions. I've had my disagreements with Sabato over the years, but his record has been mostly on the money. In particular, he has accurately captured the story of the African American vote for the last generation. He has written over twenty books, including *Feeding Frenzy: Attack Journalism and American Politics* (Baltimore: Lanahan Publishers, 2000) and *Pendulum Swing* (Upper Saddle River, NJ: Pearson, 2011). His latest book is *The Kennedy Half-Century: The Presidency, Assassination, and Lasting Legacy of John F. Kennedy* (New York: Bloomsbury USA, 2013).

77 *An editorial in*: "A Desperate Chichester," editorial, *Virginian-Pilot*, October 5, 1985.

81 *To those who said*: Fred Barnes, "The Wilder Card," *New Republic*, September 1985.

84 *The rightward swing*: Frank B. Atkinson, *Virginia in the Vanguard: Political Leadership in the 400-Year-Old Cradle of American Democracy, 1981–2006* (Lanham, MD: Rowman & Littlefield, 2006).

85 *According to*: Frank B. Atkinson, *Virginia in the Vanguard: Political Leadership in the 400-Year-Old Cradle of American Democracy, 1981–2006* (Lanham, MD: Rowman & Littlefield, 2006).

85 *And the centerpiece*: Donald P. Baker, "Virginia's One Man TV Cop Show," *Washington Post*, November 16, 1985.

88 *There were signs*: Daniel J. Sharfstein, "The Secret History of Race in the United States," *Yale Law Journal*, 2003.

89 *As Sabato*: Larry Sabato, "The 1985 Statewide Election in Virginia: History Quietly Writ Large," newsletter, University of Virginia Institute of Government, January 1986.

90 *It was a decisive*: Michelle Williams, "Byrd's Grip Broken, Democrats Exalt," *Richmond Times-Dispatch*, November 6, 1985; John Dillin, "Grandson of a Slave Alters the Character of Southern Politics," *Christian Science Monitor,* November 14, 1985; Barry Sussman, "Hidden Racial Attitudes Distorted VA Polls," *Washington Post*, November 28, 1985.

91 *God knew I had*: Margie Fisher, "Wilder Blasts Robb, National Party," R*oanoke Times and World-News*, April 5, 1986.

92 *After the election*: "Credit Others, Wilder Aide Says," Richmond News Leader, November 18, 1985; Guy Friddell, "Off the Record: Robb's, Wilder's Political Careers Intertwined Like Wisteria Vines," *Richmond News Leader*, January 10, 1986.

92 *As a result*: Tom Sherwood, "Wilder Takes Up Senate Gavel," *Washington Post*, January 14, 1986.

Chapter Six: Virginia Is Ready

95 *The "Anyone But . . . "*: Margaret Edds, *Claiming the Dream: The Victorious Campaign of Douglas Wilder of Virginia* (New York: Workman Publishing, Algonquin Books of Chapel Hill, 1990). Edds covered Virginia politics for the *Virginian-Pilot/Ledger-Star* and was one of the sharpest reporters on the beat.

99 *I was buoyed*: David R. Jones, *Racism as a Factor in the 1989 Gubernatorial Election of Doug Wilder* (Lewiston, NY: Edwin Mellen Press, 1991).

99 *Marshall Coleman*: Steve Haner, "Coleman Says Poll Shows He Can Win," *Richmond Times and World-News*, April 16, 1985; Cummings, "Wilder More Moderate as an Insider," *Richmond News Leader*, April 10, 1989.

101 *My presumptive nomination*: Nancy Cook, "Wilder's Nomination to Draw National Press," *Daily Press*, June 3, 1989.

105 *Since April*: Richard Brisbin Jr., *A Strike Like No Other Strike: Law and Resistance during the Pittston Coal Strike of 1989–1990* (Charlottesville: University of Virginia Press, 2010); Ray Garland, "Pittston Coal Miners' Strike Puts Candidates in a Non-Win Situation," *Daily Press*, August 8, 1989.

107 *As I was finishing*: B. Drummond Ayres Jr., "Virginia Beach Is Quiet after Violence," *New York Times*, September 5, 1989.

109 *By October*: Margaret Edds, *Claiming the Dream: The Victorious Campaign of Douglas Wilder of Virginia* (New York: Workman Publishing, Algonquin Books of Chapel Hill, 1990); Fred Barnes, "Republicans Miscarry Abortion," *American Spectator*, 1990.

111 *As a sign*: "Wilder Sells Vacant Row House," *Free Lance-Star*, January 14, 1986.

111 *Through it all*: David Schribman, "The New South: Now Vastly Changed, Virginia May Choose a Black as Governor—As Wilder Takes on Coleman, Race Is Rarely Mentioned, Never Quite Forgotten," *Wall Street Journal*, October 11, 1989.

112 *Days before*: Kent Jenkins Jr., "Armed with Audacity, Wilder Elbows His Way to Brink of History," *Washington Post*, October 22, 1989; B. Drummond Ayres Jr., "The 1989 Election: The Virginia Contest Man in the News: Lawrence Douglas Wilder; From Confrontation to Conciliation," *New York Times*, November 8, 1989.

113 *Race was not*: Drummond Ayres, "Virginia Contest Avoids Race Issue—But Harsh Words Are Plentiful in a Campaign That Could Elect a Black Governor," *New York Times*, September 18, 1989.

114 *It would be disingenuous*: Eric Sundquist, "The Election Polls Were Wrong, but Why?," *Richmond Times-Dispatch*, November 9, 1989; David R. Jones, *Racism as a Factor in the 1989 Gubernatorial Election of Doug Wilder* (Lewiston, NY: Edwin Mellen Press, 1991). In 2009, Daniel J. Hopkins of Harvard University published an article suggesting that the Wilder effect virtually disappeared in more recent elections, citing the elections of Deval Patrick and Harold Ford Jr. as examples. But he cautioned that the disappearance could be temporary, depending on

the state of race relations. His article "No More Wilder Effect, Never a Whitman Effect: When and Why Polls Mislead about Black and Female Candidates" was published by the Southern Political Science Association in 2009.

113 *Larry Sabato*: Larry J. Sabato, "Virginia Governor's Race, 1989," *University of Virginia Newsletter*, Weldon Cooper Center for Public Service, July 1989 and January 1990.

115 *January 14 was*: "Wilder Sworn In as Virginia's Governor," *New York Times*, January 14, 1989.

119 *I was elated*: As a historical note, although I was the first elected black governor, I wasn't the first black governor in the country. That would be Pinckney Pinchback, who was briefly the governor of Louisiana. Pinkney was born in 1837, the son of a white man and a slave mother who was later freed. In 1868, he was elected to the Louisiana Senate and became president pro tempore. When the governor died, he became lieutenant governor and was governor for a month and a half in 1872 when the governor went through an impeachment trial.

Chapter Seven: In the Saddle

123 *Out of necessity*: Michael Hardy, "Wilder Calls for Tighter Fiscal Policy, Rules Out Tax Increase or Bond Issue," *Richmond Times-Dispatch*, January 16, 1990.

124 *However, the media*: Susan Schindehette, "Pat Kluge Gets $1.6 Million a Week in Her Record Divorce Settlement, but the Romantic Rumors Are Wilder," *People*, July 23, 1990.

125 *That's how I*: B. Drummond Ayres Jr., "Wiretapping Controversy Fuels Va. Politicians' Feud," *New York Times*, June 12, 1991; Michael Ross, "Robb's Career in Peril as Feud With Wilder Heats Up: Virginia: Governor Cites Memo, Says 'Smear' Was Used to Draw Attention from the Scandals Surrounding the Senator," *Los Angeles Times*, May 23, 1992.

126 *A Mason-Dixon*: Bob Kamper, "Poll: Robb a Loser vs. Coleman, Wilder, North, Trible," *Daily Press*, June 12, 1993.

130 *Evaluating the role*: Frank B. Atkinson, *Virginia in the Vanguard: Political Leadership in the 400-Year-Old Cradle of American Democracy, 1981–2006* (Lanham, MD: Rowman & Littlefield, 2006).

131 *In New Hampshire*: Clarence Page, "Representation: Perpetuating America's Guilty Denial about Racism," *Chicago Tribune*, July 27, 1993.

133 *In the company of*: Mandela's inspiring memoir *Long Walk to Freedom* (Boston: Little, Brown, 2008) was a testament to his humility and integrity. I was deeply affected by Mandela's death in 2013 at the age of ninety-five and wrote about him on my website, http://wildervisions.com, "The World Lost a Voice of Reason, Compassion."

134 *Perhaps the most*: Make no mistake. The huge lobby proclaiming Coleman's innocence was wrapped around an ideal opposing the death penalty. Coleman was a convenient poster boy. But when his guilt was proved by DNA, his supporters were devastated. The story is told in a riveting piece by Glenn Frankel, "Burden of Proof," *Washington Post*, May 14, 2006.

136 *When he was*: In 2007, Virginia agreed to pay Washington a settlement of $1.9 million for wrongful conviction. By that time, Washington was forty-six years old, married, and working as a maintenance man.

138 *As a sad*: Editorial Board, "Repealing a Gun Law That Worked," *Washington Post*, February 13, 2012; Laura Vozzella, "McDonnell Signs Bill Lifting One-Handgun-a-Month Limit," *Washington Post*, February 28, 2012.

139 *The stadium fight*: John Harris and Robert F. Howe, "Cooke, Wilder Give Up on Stadium," *Washington Post*, October 15, 1994.

141 *By the time*: John F. Harris, "Wilder Escorts Terry to Norfolk Churches; Governor Is Cheered in 1st Joint Appearance," *Washington Post*, October 25, 1993.

142 *One of my*: "Governor Wilder Grants Clemency to Iverson," *Daily Press*, December 31, 1993. A 2010 documentary film titled *No Crossover: The Trial of Allen Iverson* explored the case. It was produced and directed by Steve James for Kartemquin Films.

143 *Earlier in*: Donald P. Baker and Peter Baker, "Governor Wilder Quits Race for Senate: Wilder Reviews 4 Years in Office, Declares There Will Be 'No Sequel,'" *Washington Post*, January 13, 1994.

Chapter Eight: The Race Goes On

145 *Larry Sabato would call it*: Larry J. Sabato, "The 1994 Election in Virginia: The Senate Race from Hell," *University of Virginia Newsletter*, the Weldon Cooper Center for Public Service, March 1995.

147 *Soon after I*: Michael Janofsky, "The 1994 Campaign: In Senate Race, Robb Attacks North for Endorsing Display of Confederate Flag," *New York Times*, September 24, 1994.

148 *Mainstream Republicans*: Bob Kemper, "Nancy Reagan Calls North a Liar: Attacks Taking Toll, Analysts Contend," *Daily Press*, October 29, 1994.

151 *Once I made*: Chris L. Jenkins, "Wilder Triumphs in Mayor's Race: After Charter Change Former Governor Is Elected to Lead Troubled Home Town," *Washington Post*, November 3, 2004; Rob Gurwitt, "Wilder's Last Crusade," *Governing*, June 2005, www.governing.com; "NPR Profile: Douglas Wilder, Mayor-Elect of Richmond, Virginia," *All Things Considered*, December 30, 2004.

152 *But undoubtedly*: Lisa A. Bacon, "Famous Mayor under Fire in Virginia," *New York Times*, October 21, 2007.

153 *In spite of*: Jones, Will, "Wilder Had Hits, Misses as Richmond Mayor," *Richmond Times-Dispatch*, December 28, 2008.

154 *Then came a*: Benjamin Wallace-Wells, "The Great Black Hope: What's Riding on Barack Obama"?, *Washington Monthly*, November 2004.

155 *Bennett had just written*: Lerone Bennett Jr., *Forced into Glory: Abraham Lincoln's White Dream* (Chicago: Johnson Publishing, 2000).

157 *After the election*: John Hellemann and Mark Halperin, *Game Change: Obama and the Clintons, McCain and Palin, and the Race of a Lifetime* (New York: Harper, 2010).

158 *The disastrous*: Cheryl W. Thompson, Krissah Thompson, and Michael A. Fletcher, "Gates, Police Officer Share Beers and Histories with President," *Washington Post*, July 30, 2009.

159 *The unfair firing*: Shirley Sherrod, *The Courage to Hope: How I Stood Up to the Politics of Fear* (New York: Atria, 2012).

159 *Two years into*: Glen Ford, "Obama Humiliates the Black Caucus and They Pretend Not to Notice," *Black Agenda Report*, September 28, 2011.

160 *One skirmish*: Jonathan Martin, "Douglas Wilder Cool to Barack Obama's Overture in Virginia Governor's Race," *Politico*, July 24, 2009.

161 *That wasn't reason*: Paul Goldman, "McDonnell/Deeds vs. Wilder/Cullen on Guns. Who's Right?," *Blue Virginia*, February 7, 2012.

162 *Time and again*: L. Douglas Wilder, "Obama Needs a Staff Shakeup," *Politico*, February 9, 2010. A little more than a year into Obama's term, I was already speaking openly for a need for a recalibration.

166 *I had always*: Frank Green, Olympia Meola, and Jim Nolan, "Jury Finds Former Governor Bob McDonnell Guilty on Multiple Counts," *Richmond Times-Dispatch*, September 4, 2014.

167 *For this reason*: Ashley Monfort, "McDonnell Character Witnesses Plead for Leniency," NBC-12, January 6, 2015.

Chapter Nine: Reclaiming the Devil's Half Acre

172 *On the island*: Errol Barnett, "Senegal's Scenic Island Exposes Horrors of Slave Trade," CNN, February 23, 2012.

173 *How many people*: Stephen E. Ambrose, "Founding Fathers and Slaveholders: To What Degree Do the Attitudes of Washington and Jefferson toward Slavery Diminish Their Achievements?," *Smithsonian*, November 2002.

175 *By 2012*: Pamela Gould, "Slavery Museum's Future in Doubt," *The Free Lance Star*, February 21, 2009; Susan Svrluga, "Former Va. Gov. L. Douglas Wilder's Slavery Museum Project Stalled in Fredericksburg," *Washington Post*, September 18, 2012.

175 *Our proposed location*: Rob Nieweg and Brent Leggs, "Historic Places as Sites of Conscience: Shockoe Bottom's Potential to Change Society," *Huffington Post*, January 20, 2015; Doug Wilder, "Locate the Slavery Museum in Shockoe," *Wilder Visions*, March 3, 2014, http://wildervisions.com; Doug Wilder, "Correctly Telling ALL the History of Schockoe," *Wilder Visions*, June 7, 2014, http://wildervisions.com.

176 *After he was*: Doug Wilder, "U.S. National Slavery Dream Becomes Closer," *Wilder Visions*, December 1, 2013, http://wildervisions.com.

176 *Today, we are*: Press conference, National Slavery Museum, May 8, 2014, http://wildervisions.com.

176 *We can more*: Cynthia Jacobs Carter, ed., *Freedom in My Heart: Voices from the United States National Slavery Museum* (Washington, DC: National Geographic Books, 2009).

177 *In 2010*: Editor, "Texas School Board Approves Controversial Textbook Change," *Need to Know*, PBS, May 23, 2010.

177 *A similar effort*: Trymaine Lee, "Tea Party Groups in Tennessee Demand Textbooks Overlook U.S. Founder's Slave-Owning History," *Huffington Post*, January 23, 2012.

177 *Representative Michele*: Glen Kessler, "The Fact Check: Bachmann on Slavery and the National Debt," *Washington Post*, January 28, 2011. It bears noting that as Bachmann's example of an antislavery founding father, she cited John Quincy Adams, our sixth president. Adams was not a founding father, having been only nine years old in 1776.

Chapter Ten: Ringing the Bell

179 *In the early*: W. E. B. Du Bois, "The Talented Tenth," in *The Negro Problem: A Series of Articles by Representative Negroes of Today* (New York, 1903), www.webdubois.org.

180 *After my term*: Judson L. Jeffries, *Virginia's Native Son: The Election and Administration of Governor L. Douglas Wilder* (West Lafayette, IN: Purdue University Press, 2000).

180 *Yet even as*: David Welna, "Why Have So Few African Americans Been Elected to the Senate?," NPR, October 13, 2013.

184 *Our efforts culminated*: "Senate Committee Hearing Testimony on Plight of Black Men Gets Eye-Opening Lecture," *Jet*, June 10, 1991.

188 *From the pulpit*: Curtiss Paul DeYoung, "The Role of the Black Church in the Civil Rights Movement," www.academia.edu.

188 *When I heard*: Braden Goyette, "Stark Racial Disparities in Ferguson, Missouri, the Town Where Michael Brown Was Shot," *Huffington Post*, August 12, 2014.

190 *I have been*: Virginia Commonwealth University, L. Douglas Wilder School of Government and Public Affairs, www.vcu.edu.

190 *In 2013*: My graduation speech to the Ailes Apprentices is at http://wildervisions.com.

191 *In the 2014*: Dave Jordan, "Exit Poll Angers Some SC Voters," www.wspa.com.

192 *Whenever I can*: On December 4, 2014, in honor of the twenty-fifth anniversary of my election as governor, Virginia Commonwealth University hosted a daylong symposium to discuss my election, my administration, and a path to the future. Reporters Margaret Edds, Dwayne Yancey, Michael Hardy, and others who had spent lifetimes covering Virginia politics led panel discussions, as did Paul Goldman and Mac McFarlane. Former governors George Allen and James Gilmore also spoke. The theme of "eternal vigilance" was the underpinning of the symposium and the reception that followed. In January, the *Richmond Times-Dispatch* published a special eight-page 25th Inaugural Anniversary Section titled "History Made," reflecting on my life and career. It was observed many times that I was not the retiring kind, and that was certainly true.

ACKNOWLEDGMENTS

While I have always tried to make my own way, I have been very fortunate to have a number of people whose talents and input have helped shape me personally and professionally. It is my great pleasure to take this opportunity to recognize them.

First, this book would not have come together as successfully as it has without the support of my benevolent drillmaster Catherine Whitney, who cracked the whip increasing the specificity, timeliness, and order of the project and who lent her innumerable narrative gifts to this project; my agent Jane Dystel; my editor Eugene Brissie; my trusted advisers Cordel Faulk and J. Parker Gouchenor; and my research and administrative assistant Angelica Bega Hart. I am also grateful for the guidance of Dan Conley and to Glen Davidson for his participation and recommendations.

The great opportunity of writing a book such as this one is the chance to reflect on those who have made a significant impact on my life and helped me grow as a person. Early influencers include the many men at Dick and Percy Reid's barbershop who encouraged me to argue and support my arguments in a community of men. Many educators, including all of my elementary teachers and most in high school, especially J. R. Ransome Jr., also made a significant impact on me as a young man. In college, Dr. Limas D. Wall; Dr. Lewis O. Jeffries, who taught chemistry; Dr. Wesley Stevens, who taught calculus; and Dr. John Malcolm Ellison, the first African American president of Virginia Union University, were catalysts in shaping my early professional interests. In the military, Major Earl C. Acuff, whom I acknowledge in the book, helped me believe in the possibility that promises of fairness and equality could be fulfilled and demonstrated unparalleled leadership and vision.

Numerous people were also influential in my legal career: Roland D. Ealey and Colston A. Lewis, who wrote the letters that helped secure my admission to Howard University; Spottswood W. Robinson, who asked Thurgood Marshall to appoint me as his successor as the NAACP Legal Defense and Education Fund Inc. representative; and Professor Herbert O. Reed of Howard University Law School. These men all had a significant impact on me. While I was in law school, I also had a friend, Lewin R. Manley Jr., who was in dental school. He has remained a longtime friend, and we have maintained an understanding of race in America and its portents.

Many people were instrumental during my political career: Paul Goldman, whose incisive mind and quick grasp of political issues were invaluable in my campaigns; Senate clerk J. Shropshire; Susan Clarke Schaar, former deputy and now clerk of the Virginia State Senate; William V. Rawlings, my desk mate in the Senate who hailed from Ivor; William B. Hopkins, a fellow Korean War veteran from Roanoke; and Peter K. Babalas, senator from Norfolk. All were amiable and instructive colleagues in my political career. I want to acknowledge the help and advice of Earl Davis, experienced representative of COPE. He also gave freely of his time to the development of the clout of the Crusade for Voters. To those in my administration as governor, too numerous to list here, I thank you all as well.

As you can tell from reading this book, a passionate and enduring goal of mine is the building of a National Slavery Museum. In that effort, Vonita Foster, Bill Cosby, Sandy Robinson, William P. Jones, Vincent C. Robinson, and Vinceretta T. Chiles have each endeavored alongside me in making this dream a reality. I also want to acknowledge Harry Watkins for his benefactions as well as those who maintain the Spirit of Freedom garden.

I've always believed in the importance of education as a pathway to success; thus, I've been grateful for the support of three wonderful

Virginia universities. First, my alma mater, Virginia Union University, where a beautiful library facility was named in my honor—the first such building or facility so named and the first grantor of the many honorary degrees that I have received. At Virginia Union, President Claude O. Perkins; former board president Frank S. Royal; Rita Henderson, director of art acquisition, marketing, and development; and Selecia Gregory Allen, archivist in Special Collections, have all been tremendous assets. At Virginia Commonwealth University (VCU), where I currently lecture and where the School of Government and Public Affairs bears my name, President Michael Rao, Dean Niraj Verma, and former President Eugene Trani have been very supportive. Thanks also to the staff at VCU's Special Collections and Archives who allowed my research assistant to use their facilities in completing her duties. At Virginia State University, where I began my career in teaching, it is incumbent on me to thank Dr. Calvin M. Miller, former dean of the School of Humanities for his efforts. The support of individuals at all of these universities has been tremendous. I also want to acknowledge Howard University's School of Law for taking a chance on me (my grades were not the strongest suit in my application).

Friends and family have also paved the way for this book and so many other projects. Of course, my parents, siblings, and extended family have all played roles. So too have my children, Lynn, Larry, and Loren. It has been a profound joy to watch them grow into amazing adults and to see the promise in my grandsons, Dean and Wilder. I also must thank my friend and law partner Roger Gregory, whose wit and wisdom truly set him apart. In addition, I want to thank Dr. Robert "Bob" Holsworth, former director of the School of Government at VCU before it gained independence and the former chair of the Department of Political Science, for his continued support and friendship.

Index

About the Author

During more than fifty years of public life, L. Douglas Wilder has been at the forefront of many historic moments. In 1969, he won election to the Virginia Senate from his hometown, Richmond, and in the process became the first African American elected to that body since the end of Reconstruction. While serving in the senate, he rose to the chairmanship of several powerful standing committees during sixteen years of service. By the time he began his 1985 campaign to become Virginia's thirty-fifth lieutenant governor, Wilder was recognized as one of the commonwealth's most powerful legislators. Many pundits predicted that Virginia was not ready to elect an African American statewide official in 1985, but Wilder set out on an extensive tour that took him to all one hundred and thirty counties and cities in the commonwealth. He won the election, becoming the highest elected African American official in the country at that time.

Four years later, he again set out on a tour of the commonwealth, this time as a candidate for governor of Virginia. Again, some pundits doubted that Virginians were ready to elect a grandson of slaves as their state's chief executive. Again, voters of the commonwealth proved they were ready, choosing Wilder to serve as the sixty-sixth governor of Virginia.

During his term, Governor Wilder faced a severe budget crisis during a deep recession but managed repeatedly to balance the budget without raising taxes. Following Wilder's years as governor, he became a respected political, social, and economic commentator in addition to teaching classes at Virginia Commonwealth University.

In the early 2000s, a broad array of Richmonders reached out to Wilder and asked him to help lead an effort to reform the governing structure of the city of Richmond. After residents voted overwhelmingly to change the charter and elect a strong mayor, Wilder was elected mayor in 2004.

When Wilder retired from the office of mayor in 2009, he returned to his role as a Distinguished Professor at the L. Douglas Wilder School of Government and Public Affairs at Virginia Commonwealth University while also serving as a national commentator on public affairs.

Wilder graduated from Virginia Union University in 1951 with a degree in chemistry. He earned his juris doctorate from the Howard University School of Law in 1959. He is the father of three children, Loren, Lynn, and Lawrence Douglas Jr., and resides in Richmond, Virginia.

Website: Wilder Visions. www.wildervisions.com
Follow Doug Wilder on Facebook and on Twitter: @GovernorWilder